Human-Centered AI

Implementing Ethical Algorithms in Business Digital Ethics for Managers: Making Principled Decisions in a Data-Driven World

Dr. Ben Chuba
&
Nicci Brochard

Human-Centered AI

Implementing Ethical Algorithms in Business Digital Ethics for Managers: Making Principled Decisions in a Data-Driven World

Book Formatting by: Monisha

Book cover design by: *Billy Design*

CROSSBORDER
PUBLISHERS LLC

New York, London, Quebec

Contents

Introduction

Artificial intelligence has moved from research labs to boardrooms, quietly shaping decisions that affect customers, employees, and entire industries. Algorithms recommend which applicants are hired, which products reach consumers, and even how financial risks are calculated. These systems bring enormous efficiencies, yet they also raise questions that managers cannot ignore: Who is accountable when an algorithm discriminates? How can leaders ensure decisions are fair, transparent, and aligned with organizational values?

The promise of AI lies not only in speed and scale but in its potential to extend human judgment, rather than replace it. Human-centered AI places people at the core of design and implementation, guiding organizations to pursue innovation without sacrificing integrity. The leaders who thrive in this new landscape will be those who treat ethics as strategy, weaving responsibility into the fabric of digital transformation rather than treating it as an afterthought.

This book provides managers with practical tools, frameworks, and real-world lessons for embedding digital ethics into business practice. From understanding global standards to building internal governance, from evaluating bias in data to ensuring explainability in outcomes, the path forward requires both technical literacy and principled decision-making. The goal is not to fear algorithms, but to shape them with foresight and responsibility.

Every era of business has its defining challenge. For the data-driven age, it is learning to harness AI in ways that respect human dignity while delivering competitive advantage. The future belongs to leaders who understand that profitability and responsibility can reinforce one another. By approaching AI with clarity, care, and courage, organizations can unlock innovation while building trust that lasts.

The journey of human-centered AI begins here—with confidence that technology, guided by ethics, can serve both progress and people.

Nicci and I (Ben) thank you immensely for choosing our book. We promise you a great time ahead.

Chapter 1

The AI Revolution and the Ethics Imperative

AI's Expanding Role in Business

A rtificial intelligence has rapidly moved from the fringes of business to center stage. Once seen as experimental or niche, AI is now a driving force behind innovation and efficiency across industries. In industry after industry, AI is transforming how work gets done and how decisions are made:

- **Finance:** Banks and investment firms use AI algorithms to detect fraud, evaluate creditworthiness for loans, manage risk, and execute lightning-fast trades. Automated trading systems, for example, analyze market data in real time and make split-second decisions that would be impossible for a human trader.

- **Healthcare:** AI systems assist doctors by analyzing medical images (like X-rays or MRIs) to help detect diseases earlier and more accurately. Hospitals use machine learning to predict patient complications, optimize staffing, and even suggest personalized treatment plans based on big data. AI-driven tools are speeding up drug discovery and helping medical researchers find new cures faster.

- **Retail and Marketing:** Retailers leverage AI for personalized shopping experiences – ever notice how online stores "know" what you might want? That's AI analyzing your browsing and purchase history to recommend products and tailor promotions. Inventory management and logistics are also improved by AI predictions of demand, ensuring shelves are stocked and deliveries are routed efficiently.

- **Manufacturing and Logistics:** Factories are using AI-powered robots and quality control systems to automate production with high precision. Predictive maintenance algorithms can forecast when a machine is likely to break down and schedule repairs before a costly breakdown occurs. In logistics, AI optimizes delivery routes and supply chains, cutting costs and improving speed.

Across virtually every sector – from transportation (think self-driving vehicles and smart traffic systems) to human resources (AI tools that screen résumés) – data-driven algorithms are becoming integral to daily operations. Many routine tasks that employees used to handle manually are now augmented or handled entirely by AI. For instance, insurance companies rely on algorithms to process claims in minutes, and customer service departments deploy chatbots to answer common questions around the clock. AI doesn't just speed things up; it can uncover patterns in massive datasets that humans might miss, leading to new insights and smarter strategies.

The scale of adoption is staggering. Organizations big and small are investing in AI capabilities to gain a competitive edge. Industry forecasts predict that by the mid-2020s, the vast majority of new business software applications will include some form of AI. In other words, if a company isn't using AI yet, it's likely planning to. This widespread implementation means AI systems are increasingly making decisions that affect people's lives – whether it's approving a loan, diagnosing an illness, or deciding which advertisement a consumer sees. With AI's expanding role comes tremendous opportunity for efficiency and growth, but also a critical responsibility: ensuring that this technology is used wisely and ethically.

As AI becomes woven into the fabric of business, it amplifies both the upsides and the risks. On one hand, companies are seeing productivity gains, improved customer experiences, and solutions to problems that once seemed intractable – all thanks to intelligent algorithms. On the other hand, when AI goes wrong, it can go wrong at scale. A single flawed algorithm in a banking system, for example, could misallocate funds or deny loans to thousands of qualified customers before anyone notices. The dual nature of AI's power – its ability to do great good or cause serious harm – is why the "ethics imperative" has risen alongside the AI revolution. Business leaders are recognizing that deploying AI without careful consideration of ethical implications can backfire badly. In the next section, we'll explore why ethics matter so much in the age of AI and what can happen when those considerations are overlooked.

Why Ethics Matters for AI

With AI systems making so many decisions, the stakes are high. Deploying AI without ethical considerations can lead to serious consequences. One major risk is biased or inequitable decisions. AI algorithms learn from data, and if that data reflects unfair biases or incomplete information, the AI can end up discriminating against certain groups of people. There have been sobering real-world examples of this. In hiring, for instance, a global tech company developed an AI résumé screening tool to speed up recruitment – but they discovered it was favoring male candidates and penalizing résumés that included the word "women's," because the algorithm had learned from past hiring data dominated by men. Needless to say, that AI had to be scrapped once it was found to be unfair. In another headline-grabbing case, a new credit card's algorithm offered significantly lower credit limits to women compared to men with similar financial profiles. When a famous tech entrepreneur revealed that he got a credit limit twenty times higher than his wife's, it sparked public outcry. The incident triggered an investigation into whether the AI was biased against women. These examples show how an AI intended to streamline decisions can inadvertently reproduce or even amplify social biases – and when that happens, it's not just a glitch, it's an ethical and public relations disaster.

The loss of customer trust is another huge risk when AI behaves badly. Customers and the public expect companies to use AI responsibly. If users find out an automated system is treating them unfairly or invading their privacy, they quickly lose confidence in the brand. Think about it: would you trust a bank if you learned it was denying mortgages to qualified borrowers just because an algorithm had a biased training dataset? Probably not – you'd take your business elsewhere, and you might warn your friends and colleagues too. Trust is hard to earn and easy to lose, especially in the digital age where news of a company's missteps can spread virally on social media. A single AI misjudgment, like a tone-deaf chatbot response or a flawed product recommendation algorithm that reinforces stereotypes, can make customers feel alienated or offended. When people start seeing a company as irresponsible with AI, it can damage the brand's reputation for the long term.

That leads to the broader issue of reputational damage and even legal penalties. No company wants to wake up and find itself as the subject of the latest AI ethics scandal splashed across the headlines. The news practically writes itself when things go wrong – "Algorithm Discriminates Against Minority Applicants" or "AI Error Costs Customers Millions." Such scandals can cost companies dearly, not just in embarrassment but in real financial losses.

There's the immediate fallout – bad press, customer backlash, stock price dips – and then the aftermath, which often involves regulators and lawsuits. In some industries, using AI without regard for fairness or transparency can violate anti-discrimination laws or consumer protection regulations. Regulators are increasingly scrutinizing AI decisions: for example, authorities might investigate a biased lending algorithm for violating equal credit opportunity rules. Companies have faced fines and legal action when their AI systems were found to be unfair or when they violated privacy rights. In Europe, sweeping regulations like the proposed AI Act aim to hold organizations accountable for AI-related harms, which means businesses could incur heavy penalties if their algorithms cause unjust outcomes.

In short, ethics matter for AI because the cost of getting it wrong is so high. If an AI model is inequitable or opaque, the problem isn't merely technical – it directly affects people's lives and can lead to public scandals or loss of goodwill. On the flip side, integrating ethics from the start can be a competitive advantage. It helps ensure AI decisions are fair, transparent, and explainable, which in turn builds trust with customers and partners. Companies that take AI ethics seriously are far less likely to stumble into the kinds of pitfalls that make negative headlines. In a world where "move fast and break things" was once a popular mantra in tech, businesses are realizing that when it comes to AI, a reckless approach can break something very important: public trust. Getting it right from the start is critical – it's far better to invest in ethical practices upfront than to try to repair damage after an AI fiasco. By proactively addressing issues like bias, privacy, and accountability, companies protect themselves and the people they serve, ensuring that AI's expanding role in business remains a positive one.

Defining Human-Centered AI

So what exactly do we mean by "human-centered AI"? In a nutshell, it means designing and deploying AI systems with people's needs, values, and well-being at the core. Rather than asking "How can we get the machine to do everything?", a human-centered approach asks, "How can this AI help people do things better?" The idea is that technology should serve humans, not the other way around.

Practically speaking, human-centered AI is about creating algorithms and models that augment human decision-making, not undermine or replace it. Think of AI as a smart assistant: it can crunch numbers, find patterns, and offer suggestions, but ultimately it should empower people to make better choices – not make those choices for them without oversight.

A human-centered AI system is built around key ethical principles that keep it aligned with human values. Three of the fundamental principles often cited are fairness, transparency, and accountability. Let's break those down in plain language:

- **Fairness:** The AI should treat people fairly and avoid bias. This means making sure the algorithm doesn't systematically favor or disfavor any group unjustly. If an AI is screening job candidates or evaluating loan applications, a fair system would give everyone equal opportunity, basing decisions on relevant criteria rather than on factors like gender or race (especially biases that might lurk in historical data). Achieving fairness might involve carefully curating training data, testing AI outputs for bias, and continuously refining the model to correct any unintended discrimination.

- **Transparency:** The AI's decisions and workings should be as transparent or explainable as possible. In human-centered design, we don't want "black box" models where nobody (except maybe a few PhD engineers) understands how they work. Transparency means that people affected by an AI decision can get an explanation in understandable terms. For example, if an AI denies someone a loan, transparency would entail providing a clear reason – e.g. "Your application was turned down because your income was below the threshold for this product" – rather than a cryptic code or no feedback at all. Being open about how AI is making decisions helps users feel they aren't at the mercy of a mysterious algorithm; they can see the rationale behind outcomes. Transparency builds trust.

- **Accountability:** There must be accountability for what the AI does. This principle is about ensuring that there are humans in the loop who take responsibility for the AI's behavior and outcomes. If an AI system makes a mistake or causes harm, a human-centered approach means the organization acknowledges it and addresses it – you can't just shrug and blame "the computer." Accountability also implies governance: setting up oversight boards, ethical guidelines, and review processes so that AI deployments are monitored and evaluated for their impact. In short, someone is answerable for the AI's actions, and there are mechanisms to correct course when needed.

Beyond these principles, human-centered AI often involves other values like privacy, user autonomy, and user experience. A human-centered design ensures the AI respects users' privacy and data rights, and that it's user-friendly and accessible to a wide range of people.

Importantly, this approach emphasizes keeping humans involved in critical decisions. For instance, an AI medical diagnosis tool might highlight likely health issues and possible treatments based on patient data, but the final call rests with the doctor and patient. They can weigh the algorithm's input alongside personal context. Similarly, an AI-driven customer service chatbot can handle common requests, but it will hand off to a human agent when queries become complex or sensitive.

The tone around human-centered AI is intentionally friendly and non-technical because these ideas aren't just for engineers – they're for everyone.

You shouldn't need a doctorate in computer science to understand when an AI is acting in your best interests. When companies talk about keeping AI "centered" on people, they mean designing systems that *any user* can interact with comfortably and confidently.

For example, a finance app using AI to give budgeting advice would be human-centered if it explains its recommendations clearly and allows the user to adjust or override them, rather than just dictating a budget with no input. The goal is for AI to feel like a helpful colleague or tool, not a mysterious overlord.

In essence, human-centered AI is about balancing innovation with empathy and common sense. Yes, AI can process data on a superhuman scale, but the reason it exists in a business context is to serve human goals – whether that's helping customers, supporting employees, or benefiting society. By defining success not just in terms of an algorithm's accuracy or efficiency but also in terms of human satisfaction and well-being, companies can ensure their AI initiatives stay aligned with what truly matters.

This sets the stage for managers and leaders to play a crucial role – they are the ones who must champion these values and make sure the AI revolution doesn't lose sight of the people it's meant to help.

Managers as Ethical Stewards

If human-centered AI is the destination, how do we get there? This is where leadership comes in. Business managers and executives have to act as ethical stewards for AI within their organizations. Interestingly, most leaders already *say* that AI ethics matters to them – but far fewer have translated that into concrete practices. According to a recent industry survey, about 79% of executives acknowledged that AI ethics is important to their company's success, yet less than one in four have actually implemented an internal AI ethics governance program or oversight process. In other words, there's a big gap between awareness and action. It's one thing to recognize, "Yes, we need to use AI responsibly," and quite another to put guidelines, teams, and tools in place to make sure that happens day-to-day.

Why is it crucial for managers to take the lead here? Because ethical AI doesn't happen by accident – it requires deliberate choices and policies set at the top. Engineers and data scientists can build algorithms, but managers set the objectives, the constraints, and the company culture that determine how those algorithms are used. If a company ends up in a scandal over a biased AI, it often reflects a failure of leadership as much as a technical error. By contrast, when managers proactively champion ethical principles, they set a tone that ripples through the whole organization. Teams feel empowered to speak up about potential issues, and projects are more likely to undergo ethical reviews before launch. Essentially, leaders have the opportunity to bridge the gap between lofty principles and real-world practices.

Being an ethical steward of AI is also a smart business strategy. Companies that build ethics into their AI development are positioning themselves for long-term success. They're less likely to face the costly fallout of mistakes, and more likely to earn trust from customers, employees, and partners. Consider a manager at a healthcare company deploying an AI diagnostic tool. If she ensures that her team validates the tool for accuracy across different patient groups and sets up a process for doctors to override AI recommendations when needed, she's not just avoiding risk – she's likely improving patient outcomes and confidence in the system. That kind of due diligence might not grab headlines the way a scandal would, but it yields steady benefits: reliable AI performance, fewer failures, and a strong reputation for care and responsibility.

Moreover, regulators and governments are increasingly expecting companies to govern their AI. Managers who get ahead of regulations by establishing ethics boards or AI oversight committees can help shape the standards rather than scramble to comply later. It's akin to how companies responded to data privacy trends – the forward-thinking leaders instituted privacy policies and transparency reports before laws mandated them, which gave them a say in the conversation and a head start in adapting to new rules. With AI, a similar pattern is emerging. There's a leadership opportunity for those who take principled action early: they can influence industry best practices and even help define what "responsible AI" looks like in their field.

On a practical level, what can managers do to champion AI ethics? Here are a few steps:

- **Set clear guidelines** within their teams about what is acceptable and unacceptable when using AI. For example, require that any AI system used in decision-making is tested for bias and explainability before deployment.

- **Invest in ethics training** so that employees understand issues like bias, privacy, and security in AI. Building awareness at all levels makes ethical considerations part of the workflow, not an afterthought.

- **Establish cross-functional AI ethics committees** that include diverse perspectives (not just tech experts, but also folks from legal, HR, and representatives of the customer's point of view) to review important AI projects. A variety of viewpoints can catch ethical issues others might miss.

- **Encourage an open culture** where raising ethical concerns is welcomed, not seen as hindering innovation. If a data scientist or any team member can say, "I'm worried this model might not be fair to everyone," and leadership takes it seriously, that's a sign of true ethical stewardship.

It's worth noting that AI is still a relatively new frontier for many businesses in this data-driven world. Managers don't have to be AI experts to lead on ethics. What they need is a commitment to principled decision-making – the willingness to ask tough questions like "Could this algorithm harm anyone or exclude someone unfairly?" and then act on the answers. By viewing themselves as guardians of both the company's success and its values, business leaders can ensure that the AI revolution remains aligned with human interests. That not only prevents disasters but also inspires innovation that people can believe in. In sum, taking ownership of ethical AI is not just a responsibility for managers – it's also a chance to build a legacy of trust and principle in an increasingly AI-driven era.

Chapter 2

The Ethical Challenges of AI in Business

Artificial Intelligence holds great promise for businesses but also introduces profound ethical challenges. Managers and executives implementing AI must be aware of these pitfalls to make principled decisions. In this chapter, we explore four major ethical challenges of AI in business – bias and discrimination, opacity and explainability, privacy and data misuse, and accountability and liability – each with real-world case studies. The tone here is practical and factual, providing insight for business leaders and interested readers alike on why these issues matter and how they pose both moral and business risks.

Bias and Discrimination in AI Systems

One of the most prominent ethical issues with AI in business is the risk of bias and discrimination. AI systems can unintentionally perpetuate human biases present in their training data. In other words, algorithms learn from historical or collected data – and if that data reflects social prejudices or imbalances, the AI may reproduce or even amplify those biases. This can result in certain groups being systematically favored or disadvantaged by automated decisions, which is both a moral problem and a business risk. For managers, an AI that discriminates can lead to public backlash, regulatory penalties, and the loss of customer trust.

A now-famous example is Amazon's experiment with an AI recruiting tool. The system was trained on ten years of resumes, most coming from men due to the tech industry's male dominance. The unintended result? The AI *taught itself* that male candidates were preferable and began penalizing resumes containing the word "women's" (for instance, resumes noting involvement in a "women's chess club"). It even downgraded graduates of women's colleges. In effect, the model learned a gender bias from historical hiring patterns. Amazon's team tried to correct the algorithm by removing explicit gendered terms from consideration, but they could not guarantee other proxies of gender wouldn't be used. Ultimately, Amazon scrapped the project entirely, recognizing the tool was not evaluating candidates in a gender-neutral way. This case highlights how even unintentional bias can creep into AI and force a company to abandon a high-tech initiative – a costly lesson in both R&D resources and public relations.

Importantly, AI bias is not limited to gender. Age discrimination has also been observed. In 2023, a tutoring company called iTutor Group faced an EEOC (Equal Employment Opportunity Commission) lawsuit after its AI recruiting software was found to automatically reject older applicants – specifically, female candidates over 55 and male candidates over 60. More than 200 qualified teachers had their applications denied solely due to an algorithmic filter on age. The company settled the case for $365,000 and agreed to implement new anti-discrimination policies. What's instructive for managers is the EEOC's stance: *"Even when technology automates the discrimination, the employer is still responsible,"* emphasized the EEOC chair. In other words, using an AI tool does not absolve a business of accountability for biased outcomes. Employers must vet their algorithms just as they would their human hiring practices – the liability for unfair treatment remains with the company.

Racial bias is another serious concern. AI systems used in healthcare and finance have shown racially skewed results. One prominent study revealed that a healthcare risk-prediction algorithm (deployed on over 200 million U.S. patients) was prioritizing care for white patients over sicker Black patients. The root cause was that the algorithm used healthcare spending as a proxy for healthcare needs – historically, less money had been spent on Black patients' care (due to systemic inequalities), so the algorithm inaccurately inferred they were lower priority. The outcome was a racially biased allocation of healthcare resources. For a business (say, an insurance company or hospital network using such an AI), this kind of bias not only harms patients but also exposes the organization to legal risks and reputational damage. No company wants headlines about an AI that discriminates against a minority group. Moreover, addressing such bias after deployment can be expensive and complex, so it's far better to prevent it through careful design and diverse data in the first place.

Even seemingly straightforward AI applications like facial recognition have demonstrated bias, underlining the need for caution. Facial recognition algorithms developed by tech companies have misidentified individuals of certain ethnicities more frequently, leading to false matches. In law enforcement use, this has resulted in *wrongful arrests* of Black citizens who were incorrectly identified by an AI. Such cases in

Detroit and New Orleans came to light, illustrating how algorithmic bias can translate into real-world injustices. For businesses developing or deploying AI (whether for security, hiring, customer analytics, or other purposes), this serves as a warning. If your AI tool unfairly targets or excludes a demographic group, you may not only harm those individuals but also face public outrage, boycotts, or civil rights lawsuits.

From these examples, the practical lesson for managers is clear: bias in AI is both an ethical lapse and a business liability. Companies should rigorously test AI systems for bias before deployment – using diverse test data and fairness audits – and remain vigilant through ongoing monitoring. If skewed outcomes are detected, teams must be prepared to intervene, retrain models with more representative data, or adjust algorithms to correct the bias. Embracing fairness as a core principle isn't just altruism; it protects the business from risk. In a data-driven world, maintaining equity and fairness in automated decisions helps preserve your brand's reputation and ensures compliance with discrimination laws. Ethical AI is, ultimately, smart business.

Opacity and Explainability: The "Black Box" Problem

Many advanced AI algorithms today operate as "black boxes" – their internal logic is so complex or opaque that even the developers may struggle to explain how a specific decision was made. This opacity poses a serious challenge in business settings. When an AI model recommends a course of action or makes an automatic decision (such as denying a loan, rejecting a job applicant, or flagging a transaction), stakeholders naturally want to know "why?". If the answer is, "We don't really know

– the AI just came up with that output," it undermines trust and accountability. People are hesitant to trust a process they don't understand, especially when high-stakes decisions are involved.

This lack of explainability isn't just a philosophical issue – it has concrete implications for businesses. Internally, managers need to justify AI-driven decisions to executives, auditors, or board members. Externally, customers and clients may demand explanations, and regulators increasingly require them. For instance, in financial services there are laws mandating that customers be given specific reasons if they are denied credit. In 2023 the U.S. Consumer Financial Protection Bureau explicitly warned lenders that using complex AI models does not excuse them from explaining decisions: *"Creditors must be able to specifically explain their reasons for [a credit] denial. There is no special exemption for artificial intelligence."*. In other words, no matter how sophisticated your AI, if it's used in lending (or similar domains), you must translate its output into clear, human-understandable reasons. Failing to do so isn't just bad customer service – it's likely a compliance violation.

The "black box" nature of many AI systems also makes it difficult for businesses to conduct "what-if" analyses or perform effective oversight. For example, if a predictive model for insurance pricing suddenly raises rates for a segment of customers, analysts need to figure out what inputs or factors led to that outcome. Traditional statistical models or simpler algorithms allow some transparency – one can usually trace which factors (like credit score, age, location) drive the decision. But a deep learning model with millions of parameters might not offer a straightforward explanation. This can leave managers in the dark about whether the decision was based on sound reasoning or if the model latched onto some spurious correlation. The inability to probe and understand the AI's reasoning can lead to blind spots where errors go unnoticed until they cause a major problem. It also makes improving the model challenging, because if you don't know why it's making mistakes, you can't easily fix them.

Moreover, opacity in AI decisions can trigger stakeholder skepticism and regulatory scrutiny. Consider the perspective of a client or the general public: if a hospital's AI system recommends against a certain treatment for a patient but offers no explanation, doctors and patients will be understandably wary. They might doubt the system's reliability and choose not to use it, negating any efficiency benefits it was supposed to bring. In the corporate sphere, a hiring or promotion algorithm that can't justify its choices could be seen as arbitrary or biased. Regulators in Europe and elsewhere are responding to these issues. The upcoming EU AI Act, for example, places a strong emphasis on transparency and might effectively require that high-risk AI systems have some level of explainability. The logic is that *if* AI is being used in decisions that affect people's rights or livelihoods, then those people (or oversight bodies) have a right to understand the basis of the decisions. Transparency laws are emerging to ensure algorithms can be audited and explained, precisely to prevent hidden biases or errors from going unchecked.

For managers, the practical advice is to prioritize explainability in AI projects whenever possible. This might mean choosing slightly less complex models that offer more transparency, or investing in Explainable AI (XAI) tools that can shed light on a complex model's workings. For instance, there are techniques that highlight which factors had the most influence on a particular AI decision (like SHAP values or LIME in machine learning). By implementing such tools, a company can provide a rationale: e.g., "The loan was denied primarily because the applicant's debt-to-income ratio was too high relative to our threshold," rather than "The computer said no." Adopting explainability not only helps in building trust with users and customers (who feel more comfortable knowing the reasoning), but it also helps internally – your data science team and risk managers can better understand and correct the AI's behavior. In summary, while cutting-edge AI models can be very powerful, business leaders must balance accuracy with interpretability. An AI decision, no matter how accurate, is of limited value if you cannot convince others of its legitimacy or if you can't diagnose its failures. In a world of increasing accountability, being able to explain your AI's decisions is quickly becoming not just a bonus, but a requirement for doing business in a data-driven environment.

Privacy and Data Misuse

AI systems often hunger for data – large amounts of detailed data are what fuel many machine learning models. In a business context, this can mean using troves of personal information about customers, employees, or the public. Privacy and data misuse thus become paramount ethical challenges. Managers must grapple with questions of consent, data protection, and the potential for AI to be used in ways people never expected when they handed over their information. Not only is mishandling personal data unethical, it can also violate laws and erode public trust irreparably.

A cautionary tale in this realm is the Facebook–Cambridge Analytica scandal. In 2018, it came to light that Cambridge Analytica, a political consulting firm, had harvested data from millions of Facebook users without proper consent – data that was then used to profile voters and target political ads. The data was obtained via a seemingly innocuous personality quiz app, which collected not just the quiz-taker's info but also their friends' Facebook data. This massive privacy breach affected an estimated 87 million users. The fallout was severe: Facebook faced regulatory investigations worldwide and ultimately was fined $5 billion by the U.S. Federal Trade Commission, one of the largest privacy-related fines in history. Cambridge Analytica itself went bankrupt amid the public outcry. For business leaders, the lessons here are multifold. Firstly, just because you *can* collect and utilize data with AI doesn't mean you *should* – not without clear permission and ethical safeguards. Facebook's oversight (or neglect) in protecting user data led to a monumental trust deficit; the hashtag #DeleteFacebook trended as users protested the misuse of their personal information. Secondly, regulators are now highly attuned to data misuse. Hefty fines and strict data protection laws (such as the EU's GDPR or California's CCPA) mean that privacy violations can have enormous financial consequences. In the digital age, data is an asset, but mishandling it is a serious liability.

Another contemporary example revolves around facial recognition and web-scraped images. Clearview AI, a tech company, built a controversial facial recognition database by scraping billions of images from social media and other websites without users' consent. Essentially, if you've posted a photo online, it might be in Clearview's database, which the company then markets to law enforcement agencies. This practice created what privacy advocates call a "perpetual police lineup" of citizens who never agreed to such use of their photos. Privacy regulators around the world have slammed Clearview's approach. In Australia, for instance, the government found Clearview had breached privacy laws by collecting Australians' face images without consent and ordered the company to cease collecting and delete the data. Clearview has also faced fines in Europe (for example, the UK's data authority fined it £7.5 million and ordered data deletion) and a slew of negative press. The Clearview case shows how *AI-driven data misuse* – even if technically impressive – can be seen as a gross violation of societal norms and individual rights. Businesses considering web scraping or mass data aggregation techniques must tread carefully. Reputation is at stake: no company wants to be the next headline for invasive AI practices. Public trust, once lost, is hard to regain.

Beyond these high-profile cases, privacy concerns permeate many AI projects. AI in retail analyzes customer purchase histories, location data, even in-store video to personalize marketing – but are customers aware and comfortable with this level of surveillance? Healthcare AI might train on patient records – but are proper anonymization and patient consent in place? Even employee data isn't off-limits: some firms use AI to monitor workers' productivity or communications, raising questions about workplace privacy and consent. The Cambridge Analytica and Clearview stories serve as stark reminders that abusing data can lead to legal penalties and public fury. They underscore the need for ethical data governance. Managers should enforce strict policies on data collection: obtain clear consent, collect only what is needed for a defined purpose, and ensure robust security against leaks or breaches. Data used for AI should be anonymized where possible to protect identities. It's also wise to implement data ethics reviews for AI initiatives – essentially, think through the worst-case privacy scenarios before they happen. Ask questions like, "Could this AI's use of data be seen as creepy or intrusive by our customers? Are we prepared to explain and justify our data practices if they become public?" If there's discomfort in answering, that's a sign to rethink the approach.

In sum, respecting privacy is not just a legal obligation but a strategic imperative. Businesses live and die by their reputation. Demonstrating to consumers that you handle their data with care can be a competitive advantage, fostering loyalty and goodwill. Conversely, if people suspect your AI is spying on them or exploiting their information, they will flee to competitors and regulators will come knocking. The age of AI doesn't change the fundamental dictum of the digital economy: trust is everything. And to maintain trust, companies must treat personal data with the utmost respect and transparency.

Accountability and Liability for AI Decisions

When an AI system makes a wrong or harmful decision, who is held responsible? This question of accountability and liability is one of the thorniest ethical challenges in AI deployment. In traditional operations, if an employee makes a mistake, you can address it with that employee (retrain, discipline, etc.), and if a product is defective, consumers can hold the manufacturer liable. But with AI, the decision may not be directly traceable to one human actor – it might be the result of a complex algorithm's autonomous functioning. This can create confusion and gaps in responsibility, which are dangerous both legally and ethically. Managers cannot afford to deploy AI without clarity on accountability; otherwise, when something goes wrong, the finger-pointing could be endless (and costly).

Consider the scenario of an autonomous vehicle accident. In 2018, a self-driving test car operated by Uber struck and killed a pedestrian in Tempe, Arizona – the first known pedestrian fatality caused by a self-driving vehicle. The immediate question was: who is to blame? The autonomous system was in control at the time of the crash, but a human safety driver was behind the wheel as a fallback. After investigation, Arizona prosecutors decided *not to charge Uber the company* with liability in the criminal case, instead charging the safety driver (who had been distracted at the moment of impact) with negligent homicide. In other words, the individual behind the wheel bore the brunt of legal responsibility, not the corporation or the AI developer. However, the U.S. National Transportation Safety Board (NTSB) had a more nuanced take: federal investigators noted that while the driver was indeed inattentive, Uber's own lapses contributed to the tragedy – the vehicle's AI failed to identify the pedestrian correctly and the company had deactivated a key safety feature (automatic emergency braking) in the test vehicle. They also criticized the lack of adequate safety culture and oversight in Uber's self-driving program. This example shows the murkiness of AI accountability: legally the fallback driver was held accountable, but in reality multiple parties shared responsibility – the developers who designed a flawed system, the managers who decided to turn off safeguards, perhaps even regulators who didn't impose stricter testing standards. For businesses, it's a cautionary tale: if you deploy AI (like a self-driving car or any autonomous tool), you need clear protocols on who monitors it and who is answerable if it fails. Otherwise, when incidents occur, it could result in public blame on the company even if the law isn't immediately clear, and prolonged legal battles or reputational damage can follow.

Another area to think about is AI in financial decisions. Imagine an AI-driven trading algorithm at an investment firm that suddenly goes haywire and causes massive losses by making a series of bad trades in seconds. This is not far-fetched – such incidents have occurred with algorithmic trading. If an AI "autonomously" loses $100 million, who is liable to the clients or the firm? The developers who coded the algorithm? The portfolio manager who deployed it? The CEO of the firm? Without predetermined answers, it will be chaos trying to assign blame after the fact. Similarly, if an AI used in lending or hiring results in a discriminatory impact (say it unintentionally redlines minority neighborhoods for loans, or filters out certain demographic job candidates), regulators will ask: Who approved and oversaw this AI? Companies have already faced lawsuits for such outcomes, and one can't simply shrug and blame the computer. The legal landscape is evolving to address these questions. Governments are starting to insist that companies actively assume responsibility for the behavior of their AI systems. In the US and UK, there have been moves to draft laws or guidance that underscore corporate accountability for AI – essentially saying that if your algorithm causes harm, your company should be on the hook just as if a human employee did. It would indeed be hypocritical (and untenable) to allow businesses to escape liability by hiding behind algorithms. In the European Union, discussions around an "AI Liability Directive" have aimed to make it easier for victims of AI-caused harm to seek compensation by reducing the burden of pinpointing a specific human fault. The reasoning is that AI's complexity and autonomy make it unfair to expect a victim to trace exactly which developer or data point led to an error. Instead, the framework would nudge responsibility onto the deployers or producers of AI, who are best placed to understand and control their systems. (As of the time of writing, these legal frameworks are still being hashed out, but the trajectory is clear – more accountability, not less.)

What can businesses do in the meantime? The answer is to set up internal AI governance and clear lines of accountability before deploying AI solutions. Practically, this means establishing roles such as an AI product owner, an ethics review board, or a designated executive responsible for AI oversight. There should be a documented chain of responsibility for each AI system: for example, a committee or officer who signs off that the AI has been tested for safety and fairness, a team assigned to monitor its decisions and intervene if issues arise, and protocols for incident response if the AI makes a harmful mistake. Forward-thinking companies are already doing this. They appoint AI ethics officers or create multi-disciplinary teams to review algorithms for potential pitfalls. They also train staff on the proper use of AI and where human judgment must remain in the loop. By fostering a culture of accountability, businesses can avoid the "not my problem" trap. As one governance expert put it, a robust AI governance structure *"outlines the roles and responsibilities of various stakeholders... fostering a culture of accountability"*. From engineers to senior management, everyone involved in an AI project should know their duty in making sure the AI is safe, compliant, and aligned with company values. If something does go wrong, this structure enables a swift and coordinated response – and it shows regulators that the company takes its oversight role seriously.

In summary, while AI might perform tasks autonomously, responsibility cannot be autonomous – it firmly rests with the humans deploying those systems. Ensuring accountability in AI isn't just about avoiding blame; it's about maintaining trust with customers, partners, and the public. People need to know that if an AI causes harm, the company will step up to make it right. By proactively defining who is answerable for AI outcomes and by putting governance in place, business leaders can navigate the liability minefield. In a data-driven world, making principled decisions includes preparing for when the data (or algorithms) go wrong. Accountability is the compass that will help businesses steer AI innovation in a direction that is not only profitable and efficient but also ethical and worthy of the public's trust.

Chapter 3
Guiding Principles for Ethical AI

Modern organizations are increasingly reliant on artificial intelligence, making it critical to ensure these systems operate in alignment with human values. This chapter explores four guiding principles for ethical AI: Fairness and Equity, Transparency and Explainability, Privacy and Security, and Accountability and Human Oversight. Each principle is discussed with practical strategies and real-world examples to illustrate why it matters. The tone remains grounded and factual, aimed at helping executives, managers, and policymakers make principled decisions in a data-driven world.

Fairness and Equity

Fairness in AI means that automated decisions are equitable – they should not systematically favor or disadvantage any particular group. In practice, this principle is about preventing bias in algorithms and ensuring all users are treated justly. AI ethics frameworks emphasize fairness as a cornerstone: AI systems should promote social justice, fairness, and non-discrimination so that their benefits are accessible to all segments of society. When AI is fair, it upholds the same ideals of equality and justice that we expect in human decision-making.

Why is fairness so important? Biased AI outcomes can perpetuate or even amplify existing social inequalities. If left unchecked, AI could unintentionally discriminate on the basis of race, gender, age, or other characteristics by mirroring biases present in historical data. For example, Amazon famously had to scrap an AI recruiting tool after discovering it systematically discriminated against women applicants – the system learned from a decade of male-dominated hiring data and taught itself to prefer male candidates, even penalizing resumes that mentioned the word "women's". In the financial sector, there were high-profile claims that Apple's credit card AI offered lower credit limits to women than to men with similar profiles. These real-world cases (in hiring and lending, respectively) highlight how algorithmic bias can lead to unfair outcomes with serious consequences for people's livelihoods. AI ethics, in this sense, is fundamentally about social justice in automated decisions – using technology in a way that does not reinforce prejudice or deny opportunities to certain groups.

To implement fairness, organizations should proactively test algorithms for biased outcomes and take steps to mitigate any inequities found. This involves scrutinizing both data and model behavior. Datasets used for training AI must be representative of the population; if your data skews toward one group, the model's predictions will too. Likewise, models should be evaluated across different demographic slices to ensure consistent performance. Below are some strategies to promote fairness in AI systems:

- **Use representative data:** Carefully examine training datasets to verify they reflect the diversity of the real population. Fill gaps or rebalance data as needed to avoid under-representing groups.

- **Measure outcomes across groups:** During model development and testing, analyze performance for subpopulations (e.g. by gender, ethnicity, age) to check that error rates and outcomes are equitable. If the AI is much less accurate for a certain group, this signals a fairness issue.

- **Mitigate bias in design:** Incorporate fairness constraints or bias mitigation techniques in the modeling process. This could mean selecting algorithms that have fairness objectives or adjusting decision thresholds to reduce disparate impact.

- **Include diverse perspectives:** Consult with domain experts, ethicists, or social scientists when designing AI for high-stakes decisions. A diverse team is more likely to anticipate how an algorithm might unintentionally disadvantage a group.

- **Continuous monitoring and audits:** Even after deployment, monitor AI outcomes for signs of drift or emerging bias. Models can change behavior over time or as data evolves, so periodic fairness audits are essential. Integrating fairness checks into an organization's AI policy creates accountability for long-term equity.

By treating fairness as a must-have requirement (not merely a nice-to-have), businesses protect themselves and their stakeholders from ethical lapses. Fair AI systems inspire greater trust among users and avoid reputational risks or legal penalties associated with discrimination. In summary, the principle of fairness and equity ensures that AI augments human decision-making in a way that is inclusive and just, rather than amplifying societal biases.

Transparency and Explainability

AI systems are often criticized as *"black boxes"* whose inner workings are opaque. Transparency and explainability are guiding principles aimed at opening up that black box, making AI's decision-making processes clear and understandable. In practical terms, transparency means providing relevant information about how an AI system works – its algorithms, data sources, and decision criteria – to stakeholders. Explainability goes a step further by ensuring that the outputs or decisions of AI can be interpreted and traced to understandable causes. An executive or end-user might ask: "Why did the algorithm make this recommendation?" Explainability is about being able to answer that question in plain terms.

Opening up the black box is critical because people will not trust a machine's recommendations if they have no insight into how it reached them. Imagine a hiring AI that rejects a job candidate with no explanation, or an AI that approves one loan application but not another without stating reasons. Such opacity undermines confidence and can conceal errors or biases. On the other hand, when AI decisions are transparent, it becomes possible to scrutinize and challenge them if needed. In regulated industries like healthcare and insurance, explainability is not optional – it is often mandated by standards or laws that require knowing the basis of decisions. But even in less-regulated business domains, explainability is key to building trust and ensuring that AI supports human decision-makers rather than confounding them.

How can developers and managers make AI more explainable? One approach is to use inherently interpretable models when feasible. Simpler AI models, such as decision trees or logistic regression, can often be inspected directly – their logic is transparent by design. A decision tree, for instance, can be visualized and followed step by step to see how a conclusion was reached. By contrast, more complex techniques like deep neural networks or ensemble models (e.g. random forests) are usually black-box models: they churn data through many internal layers or transformations, making it hard even for their creators to explain exactly how inputs map to outputs. For these powerful but opaque models, organizations should deploy advanced explainability techniques. These include tools that provide post-hoc explanations – for example, by highlighting which features most influenced a particular prediction, or by generating simplified surrogate models that approximate the behavior of the complex model. Modern explainability toolkits (such as LIME, SHAP, and others) can produce visual or textual explanations for individual AI decisions, illuminating the model's "reasoning" in human-friendly terms. The goal is to give developers, managers, and affected users a window into the AI's decision process.

Analogy: Think of a complex AI model as a sealed black box making decisions. Explainability tools act as X-rays or windows into that box, revealing what factors are inside influencing the outcome. Just as a doctor would not trust a medical test without understanding how it works, business leaders should be wary of AI outputs they cannot interpret.

Making AI transparent also involves documentation and communication. Development teams should document how models are built and tested, including what data was used, what the model is intended to optimize, and known limitations or uncertainties. This documentation provides context so that others in the organization (like executives, auditors, or regulators) can understand the system's design. Moreover, transparency can be enhanced by user-facing explanations: for instance, an AI-driven lending platform might display a brief rationale to loan officers or applicants, such as "Application denied due to low income and short credit history." Such feedback not only helps the user but can also be used to double-check the decision for fairness or accuracy.

The benefits of explainable AI are substantial. First, it builds trust – when stakeholders see clear reasons for AI outputs, they are more likely to accept and adopt those recommendations. Second, it aids in problem diagnosis and model improvement. If an AI system makes a questionable decision, explainability helps engineers trace the error to a flawed assumption or data issue. Third, it enables what-if analyses; managers can explore how changing input factors would alter the outcome, which is valuable for strategic planning. Finally, transparency reinforces accountability: if AI decisions can be understood, then responsibility can be assigned and taken when errors occur. In fact, transparency is often a prerequisite for other ethical principles – for example, one cannot challenge an unfair decision or seek redress if one cannot see how that decision was made.

In summary, Transparency and Explainability are about making AI's workings visible and comprehensible. By treating AI as an assistant whose advice must be open to inspection, organizations ensure that even non-technical executives can grasp why the AI does what it does. This not only helps in complying with regulations and industry standards, but it cultivates an environment of trust and collaboration between human decision-makers and AI systems. Instead of a mysterious oracle, AI becomes a well-understood partner – a crucial shift for responsible, human-centered AI deployment.

Privacy and Security

In the rush to leverage big data and AI, organizations must not lose sight of privacy and security. Ethical AI design mandates that systems protect user privacy and secure data against misuse or unauthorized access. AI often relies on vast datasets, which may include personal, sensitive information about individuals. Respecting privacy means handling this data with care – collecting only what is necessary, safeguarding it, and using it in ways that users have consented to. Security, on the other hand, involves fortifying AI systems and their data stores against breaches or malicious attacks. These twin principles are linked: a failure in security (like a data breach) directly results in a privacy violation.

One cannot overstate the importance of privacy in maintaining user trust. Customers, employees, and the public expect that their personal information will not be exploited or exposed. Laws and regulations around the world underscore this expectation. The European Union's General Data Protection Regulation (GDPR), for example, requires organizations to obtain informed consent for personal data use and to implement strong data protection measures; similar laws exist or are emerging in many jurisdictions. Violating privacy not only harms individuals but also exposes businesses to legal penalties and reputational damage. A stark reminder came in 2024, when Italy's data protection authority fined the city of Trento €50,000 – the first Italian municipality penalized for an AI-related privacy breach. In that case, the city had used AI surveillance tools that collected video, audio, and social media data without properly anonymizing individuals or limiting data sharing. Regulators found this violated GDPR's requirements for transparency and data minimization, ordered all improperly collected data to be deleted, and signaled a get-tough approach on AI privacy violations. The lesson for businesses is clear: weak privacy practices can quickly erode customer trust and invite regulatory action.

Security is closely intertwined with privacy. If an AI system is not secure, hackers or insiders could steal personal data or even manipulate the AI's behavior. Unfortunately, data breaches are on the rise, with one report logging 1,862 data breaches in 2021 – a 23% increase over the previous record high. Such breaches not only carry direct financial costs (fines, remediation, etc.) but also cause severe reputational damage, as people lose confidence in a company's ability to safeguard information. Moreover, certain AI-specific attacks pose novel risks. For example, researchers have shown they could subtly alter inputs (like placing small stickers on a road) to confuse a self-driving car's AI, causing dangerous behavior. Other adversaries might poison training data or steal model parameters. These scenarios demonstrate why robust security must be a foundational principle when deploying AI, especially in critical applications.

To uphold privacy and security, organizations should adopt a privacy-by-design and security-by-design approach in their AI projects. Concretely, this means implementing measures such as:

- **Data minimization and anonymization:** Collect only the data that is truly needed for the AI's purpose, and whenever possible, remove or obfuscate personal identifiers. Techniques like anonymization or pseudonymization help protect individual identities in the dataset.

- **User consent and transparency:** Obtain clear consent from users for data collection and AI use, and be transparent about how data is used. Users should be informed when AI is involved in decisions about them. Honoring individuals' rights (like the ability to access or delete their data) is part of ethical data handling.

- **Secure data storage and transfer:** Store data using strong encryption and protect it during transmission. Limit access to data on a strict need-to-know basis – an approach known as the principle of least privilege, where each system or team member only accesses the minimum data necessary for their role. Rigid access controls and logging can prevent and detect unauthorized data access.

- **Regulatory compliance:** Stay up-to-date with relevant regulations (GDPR, consumer privacy acts, sector-specific data laws) and incorporate those requirements into AI system design and corporate policies. Compliance is not just a legal formality; it provides a well-defined baseline for privacy and security practices that significantly reduce risk.

- **Continuous security testing:** Treat AI systems like any other mission-critical software by conducting regular security assessments. This includes threat modeling (anticipating how an adversary might attack), penetration testing, and even "red team" exercises where internal experts attempt to break the AI system's defenses. By probing for vulnerabilities, organizations can fix weaknesses before they are exploited.

- **Incident response plans:** Despite best efforts, breaches or failures can happen. Having a clear response plan – including user notifications, system shutdown protocols, and remediation steps – is part of being ethically prepared. How a company handles a privacy or security incident can make a big difference in public perception and harm mitigation.

By embedding privacy and security considerations throughout the AI development lifecycle, managers ensure that their AI initiatives do not become ticking time bombs. Instead, robust data protection becomes a competitive advantage, as customers gravitate towards businesses they can trust with their information. In an age of frequent cybersecurity threats and growing privacy awareness, ethical AI means AI that keeps personal data safe and confidential, thereby safeguarding the dignity and rights of individuals.

Accountability and Human Oversight

No AI system should operate without clear accountability and appropriate human oversight. This principle asserts that organizations must take responsibility for the behavior of their AI and maintain human control at key decision points. In practice, accountability means that there are identified people or teams who can be held answerable if an AI system causes harm or makes a serious mistake. Human oversight means that AI is not given free rein to make high-stakes decisions in isolation – humans remain "in the loop" to guide the AI, review its outputs, and intervene when necessary. Together, these ideas ensure that deploying AI does not mean abdicating human judgment or ethical responsibility.

One common misconception is that striving for accountability and oversight will slow down innovation or negate the benefits of automation. On the contrary, ethical AI doesn't mean no automation – it means using automation wisely with the right safeguards. Human oversight can be calibrated to the context: not every AI output needs a person's approval, but for critical decisions (such as rejecting a job applicant, diagnosing a patient, or any action with legal or life-altering implications) many organizations mandate a human review step. This kind of approach is often called a "human-in-the-loop" model. For example, a bank might use AI to flag potentially fraudulent transactions, but a human analyst makes the final determination. The AI speeds up routine analysis, while the human prevents errors or unjust outcomes. Retaining a human in the loop – ensuring AI augments rather than replaces human decision-making – is vital for maintaining accountability.

Organizational governance structures should reflect AI accountability at all levels. At the strategic level, companies are establishing AI ethics boards or committees to oversee AI deployments. These bodies review proposed AI uses, evaluate them against ethical guidelines, and monitor outcomes. On an operational level, teams need to have clear ownership: if an AI model is making customer-facing decisions, who is responsible for its performance and ethical compliance? It could be a product manager or an AI governance officer, but the role must be assigned. With clear lines of responsibility, when something goes wrong, the organization can respond quickly – whether that means fixing a technical issue, compensating an affected customer, or even shutting down a problematic system. Having auditing and reporting mechanisms is also crucial. Regular audits (internal or external) of AI systems can ensure they remain within expected ethical bounds and comply with evolving regulations. Some companies conduct bias and impact assessments on their AI annually, similar to financial audits.

Another key aspect of accountability is providing avenues for redress if AI systems cause harm or error. No AI is perfect; mistakes will happen, and when they do, those affected should have the ability to challenge and seek remedy. This is recognized in emerging AI policies – for instance, the idea of contestability: users can contest an AI-driven decision and have a human review it. Imagine a scenario where an AI denies someone a loan or a job unfairly; there should be a process for that person to appeal the decision and have a human overturn or correct it if appropriate. Redress might also include compensation or other remedies if the person suffered a loss due to an AI's mistake. Designing AI systems with record-keeping (so you can trace what the AI did and why) helps enable such reviews. Importantly, handling appeals and corrections should be seen not just as damage control but as feedback for improvement – a way to learn where the AI went wrong and how to fix it going forward.

To implement accountability and oversight in concrete terms, organizations can take the following measures:

- **Define responsibility:** Clearly assign who (which role or team) is responsible for each AI system's decisions and outcomes. This could be documented in an AI governance policy. For example, a company might state that the Head of Credit Risk is accountable for the outcomes of an AI loan approval system.

- **Human checkpoints:** Establish policies dictating when human intervention is required. Identify decisions that are too sensitive to leave solely to AI. For those, require a human sign-off or at least a manual review stage. Make it known to staff that they should question AI outputs that seem dubious, not blindly defer to them.

- **Ethical review boards:** Set up an internal committee to vet new AI projects, especially those affecting customers or employees.

This board can enforce ethical guidelines (fairness, privacy, etc.) and approve systems only when appropriate oversight and risk controls are in place.

- **Audit and evaluate:** Conduct regular audits of AI systems for compliance with ethical standards and performance benchmarks. Include independent reviewers if possible. Audits might examine whether the AI is still treating groups fairly, whether explanations to users are accurate, and whether any unintended consequences have emerged.

- **Training and awareness:** Ensure that employees understand how to work with AI responsibly. Train managers and staff on the limits of AI, bias awareness, and the procedure for overriding AI decisions. An informed team is more likely to catch issues early and use AI in an accountable manner.

- **Mechanisms for redress:** Provide customers and employees with clear ways to question or appeal AI-driven decisions. This could be as simple as a helpdesk that handles AI-related complaints or as formal as an ombudsman for algorithmic decisions. The key is that people know they can get a human hearing. Also, set up a process to rapidly correct any harmful outcomes (e.g., if an AI wrongfully rejects someone for a service, there's a fast track to make it right).

Accountability is ultimately about maintaining human responsibility in an AI-powered world. As UNESCO's global AI ethics recommendation succinctly puts it, AI systems should not displace ultimate human responsibility and accountability for decisions. In other words, no matter how autonomous or intelligent our machines become, humans must remain answerable for what they do. Embracing this principle is not about stifling innovation; it's about future-proofing innovation. When businesses build accountability and oversight into their AI, they create systems that are reliable, trustworthy, and aligned with human values. This, in turn, makes it more likely that AI initiatives will succeed, as stakeholders feel confident that there are safety nets and ethics checks in place.

In conclusion, the guiding principles of Fairness, Transparency, Privacy, and Accountability serve as a compass for any organization implementing AI. By following these principles, managers and policymakers can make sure that AI systems are not just technically effective, but also socially responsible and human-centered. In a data-driven world, such principled approaches are what will differentiate those who harness AI for broad benefit versus those who court risk and public distrust. Businesses that commit to ethical AI will find that they not only avoid pitfalls but also build better products and stronger relationships with users – a truly principled path to innovation.

Sources: The insights in this chapter draw on current best practices and research in AI ethics, including industry analyses of AI bias and fairness, expert definitions of transparency and the "black box" challenge, privacy and data protection case studies, and governance frameworks emphasizing human oversight and redress mechanisms. These principles are echoed in global guidelines like UNESCO's

Recommendation on AI Ethics, which stress that AI should uphold fairness, transparency, and human accountability. By grounding AI initiatives in these guiding principles, organizations can navigate the complex ethical terrain of today's AI applications and make principled decisions in a data-driven world.

Chapter 4

Frameworks and Standards for Responsible AI

Global Ethical AI Guidelines

Around the world, governments and international organizations have published ethical AI guidelines that converge on core principles. *Global consensus has emerged on values like fairness, transparency, accountability, and respect for human rights in AI.* For example, the European Union's High-Level Expert Group on AI released Ethics Guidelines for Trustworthy AI in 2019. These guidelines define Trustworthy AI as AI that is lawful, ethical, and robust, and they outline *seven key requirements* including human agency and oversight, technical robustness, privacy and data governance, transparency, diversity and non-discrimination, societal well-being, and accountability. In practice, this means AI systems should have human-in-the-loop controls, be secure and reliable, protect privacy, avoid bias against protected groups, benefit society at large, and include mechanisms for audit and redress. A manager reading these EU guidelines will recognize familiar themes: ensure AI augments rather than replaces human decision-making, test that models are safe and explainable, and put processes in place to avoid unfair bias or discrimination.

Another prominent example is the OECD AI Principles, adopted by dozens of countries. These were the first intergovernmental AI standards and they *promote innovative, trustworthy AI that respects human rights and democratic values.* The OECD principles emphasize inclusive growth and well-being, human-centered values and fairness, transparency and explainability, robustness and safety, and accountability. Similarly, UNESCO introduced the Recommendation on the Ethics of Artificial Intelligence (2021) as a global framework applicable to 194 member states. UNESCO's guidance is grounded in protecting human rights and dignity, calling for AI to be developed with *transparency, fairness, and human oversight* at its core. For instance, UNESCO urges that biases in AI systems be minimized and that AI should not undermine fundamental freedoms or equality. Across these international guidelines, one finds a shared foundation: AI should be designed to benefit people and society, avoid reinforcing social inequalities, be explainable to those affected, and remain under human control. This broad alignment provides a baseline for ethical AI worldwide and gives businesses a clear message about global expectations.

Common Principles in Global AI Ethics Guidelines:

- **Fairness and Non-Discrimination:** AI systems should avoid unfair bias and treat individuals equitably, preventing discrimination based on attributes like race, gender, or religion. This often entails careful selection of training data and bias testing.

- **Transparency and Explainability:** There is consensus that AI operations need to be transparent. Stakeholders should be informed when AI is used and receive understandable explanations of AI decisions.

- **Human Agency and Oversight:** Guidelines stress that humans should remain in control. AI should augment human decision-making, not replace it entirely, and mechanisms (like human-in-the-loop reviews) should ensure human oversight of critical AI outputs.

- **Accountability:** Organizations deploying AI must be accountable for their systems' outcomes. This means establishing governance structures to audit AI, document decision processes, and provide remedies when things go wrong.

- **Privacy and Safety:** From the EU to OECD to UNESCO, protecting user privacy and ensuring AI is safe and secure are non-negotiable principles. Ethical AI guidelines call for robust cybersecurity and data governance to prevent harm.

For managers, understanding these global guidelines is valuable because they set the tone for regulations and best practices. They are not just lofty ideals; they translate into concrete expectations. For example, knowing that transparency is a universal principle, a manager might implement AI systems that can generate audit logs or user-friendly explanations. Realizing that fairness is emphasized globally, a business leader might mandate bias assessments in model development. In short, these international principles provide a common vocabulary and vision of Responsible AI which organizations can adopt as a foundation for their own AI ethics programs. Embracing this broad consensus is a first step in making AI initiatives human-centered and trustworthy by design.

Government Regulations and Policies

While high-level guidelines set the vision, governments are increasingly codifying AI ethics into hard requirements. Around the world, policymakers are moving from principles to laws that will directly impact how companies develop and deploy AI. The landmark effort here is the European Union's AI Act, slated to be the first comprehensive legal framework for AI. The EU AI Act takes a risk-based approach: it *bans certain AI practices deemed "unacceptable risk" and imposes strict obligations on "high-risk" AI systems.* For example, the Act prohibits social scoring systems (AI that systematically rates individuals' trustworthiness based on behavior or personality) and broadly bans AI that manipulates human behavior to cause harm or that exploits vulnerable groups (like interactive toys urging children to dangerous behavior). It also outlaws indiscriminate facial recognition in public spaces for law enforcement, reflecting Europe's stance that mass biometric surveillance has no place in a democratic society. By banning these high-risk practices outright, regulators draw clear red lines that some AI applications are off-limits due to ethical or safety concerns.

For AI deemed "high-risk" but not banned, the EU AI Act will require organizations to implement a host of governance measures. High-risk AI systems (such as AI used in critical infrastructure, employment decisions, creditworthiness, education, or medical devices) must be registered in an EU database and adhere to strict compliance controls. These include conducting risk assessments and obtaining conformity certifications before deployment, maintaining detailed technical documentation, and ensuring human oversight is in place during operation. There are explicit *transparency requirements* as well – users need to be informed when they are interacting with an AI (for instance, if a chatbot is AI-driven, users should know it's not human). High-risk AI must also meet standards of accuracy, robustness, and cybersecurity to minimize chances of causing harm. In essence, the EU is mandating a thorough AI governance regime: from design to post-market monitoring, companies will need to manage and document their AI systems' safety and ethics. Non-compliance can lead to hefty fines (potentially up to 6% of global turnover, similar to GDPR penalties) and even removal of AI products from the EU market. The clear message to businesses is that proactive compliance is far wiser than scrambling later. If you plan to offer an AI-driven product in Europe – whether a recruitment algorithm or a consumer-facing AI service – you'll need to build in these controls (like bias testing, record-keeping, human review processes) from the start, rather than retrofit under regulatory duress.

Beyond Europe, other governments are also shaping AI policy, though approaches vary. In the United States, as of 2025 there is still no overarching federal AI law – no single "AI Act" equivalent at the national level. Instead, the U.S. has adopted a lighter-touch, piecemeal strategy: federal agencies use existing laws and sector-specific regulations to police AI impacts (for example, the FTC can penalize "unfair or deceptive" AI practices under consumer protection law), and authorities have issued guidance like the White House's *Blueprint for an AI Bill of Rights* (which outlines voluntary principles such as algorithmic discrimination protections and data privacy). Recent administrations have secured voluntary commitments from AI companies to address safety and ethics, rather than imposing broad mandates. In absence of a federal law, some U.S. states and cities have passed their own rules – for instance, New York City now requires bias audits for AI hiring tools. This patchwork can be challenging for businesses, as complying with AI regulations means monitoring multiple emerging rules (one city might ban AI in hiring without audits, another might require notifications to employees). *The U.S. environment thus far relies heavily on corporate responsibility and self-regulation*, though momentum is growing in Congress to consider more unified legislation. For a manager in the U.S., the key is to stay alert to guidance from regulators (like the EEOC's stance on AI in HR or the FDA's updates on AI in medical devices) and to implement best practices voluntarily. By doing so, companies not only prepare for eventual laws but also build trust with users and avoid reputational or legal pitfalls. As one survey indicated, a majority of American business leaders actually support some AI regulation – including requirements for transparency and explainability – to level the playing field and clarify the rules of the road.

Meanwhile, across Asia, AI governance approaches differ by country, but many governments thus far favor innovation-friendly guidelines over strict rules. In general, Asian economies are keen to reap AI's economic benefits and are cautious about over-regulating too soon. *Many Asian countries are taking a business-friendly approach to AI regulation, prioritizing innovation and growth over prescriptive mandates.* For example, Singapore has led with an AI governance framework and "sandbox" initiatives – rather than immediately enforce laws, Singapore provides detailed guidelines (like its Model AI Governance Framework) and allows companies to experiment in controlled environments. This helps develop best practices without stifling emerging projects. Japan has issued ethical AI guidelines that highlight principles such as transparency, societal benefit, and user assistance, but these are framed as *voluntary "soft law" recommendations*, not enforceable statutes. The Japanese government encourages companies to follow these guidelines and develop self-regulation, aiming to embed ethics through cultural norms more than penalties. India has thus far focused on strategizing how AI can drive economic development and is observing how risks evolve before crafting heavy regulations. On the other hand, China presents a contrast: while fostering aggressive AI industry growth, it has begun to impose targeted regulations in line with state priorities (for instance, rules on recommendation algorithms and deepfake content, primarily to address censorship, misinformation, and security concerns). China's AI rules tend to emphasize control over data and alignment with government norms, ensuring AI doesn't destabilize social order. In summary, Asia's regulatory philosophy often leans toward *gradualism*: let the technology mature under guidance and only then solidify regulations, to avoid choking innovation prematurely.

For business leaders, this patchwork of global regulations means ethical AI can no longer be an afterthought – it's becoming a compliance issue and a strategic one. Regulations like the EU AI Act will demand new processes (e.g. *documenting AI system design decisions for audit, conducting*

regular bias and impact assessments, providing transparency tools for users).
Preparing early is crucial. Rather than waiting until a law hits, prudent
companies are proactively aligning with the strictest likely standards now.
This might involve creating an internal AI inventory to classify risk of
each application, appointing a compliance officer or taskforce for AI
oversight, and adopting frameworks (as discussed later) to systematically
manage AI risks. By building these practices today, organizations can
adapt smoothly to new rules and even influence them, instead of
scrambling at the last minute. Remember that ethical compliance is not
just about avoiding penalties; it also opens market opportunities. If your
AI product meets Europe's requirements, you signal quality and
trustworthiness that can be a competitive advantage globally. On the flip
side, ignoring the regulatory trend can leave a company exposed – legally
(fines, lawsuits), operationally (product bans or forced recalls), and
reputationally (loss of customer trust). The wise course for executives is
clear: treat AI ethics and compliance as part of your business strategy
now. As regulations tighten, those who have embedded digital ethics into
their workflow will fare far better than those trying to bolt it on later.

Manager's Checklist: Preparing for AI Regulations

1. **Inventory and Risk Assessment:** Catalog all AI systems in use
   and classify them by risk (e.g. per EU categories). Identify which
   would be considered high-risk or sensitive (hiring tools,
   customer-facing AI, etc.).

2. **Implement Oversight & Audits:** For high-stakes AI, establish
   human review processes and schedule regular ethical audits (e.g.

bias testing on algorithm outputs, fairness evaluations of datasets).

3. **Documentation and Transparency:** Maintain thorough documentation for each AI model – data sources, training methods, test results – anticipating that regulators or clients may request this. Be prepared to explain AI decisions to users in clear, non-technical terms.

4. **Staff Training and Roles:** Educate your team (product managers, developers, compliance officers) on upcoming AI laws and ethical AI practices. Assign clear responsibility for AI ethics compliance – some firms form AI governance committees or designate a "Responsible AI" lead.

5. **Monitor Legal Developments:** Keep track of AI policy developments in all jurisdictions where you operate. Adapt internal policies in advance. For instance, if new transparency rules are proposed, start building those capabilities early.

6. **Engage and Adapt:** Consider participating in industry consortia or public consultations on AI regulation. Engaging with policymakers can give insight and influence. Internally, be ready to adapt business models – for example, discontinuing an AI practice that is likely to be banned (such as intrusive biometric profiling) and investing instead in compliant innovation.

By following these steps, managers can make their organizations agile in the face of AI regulation. Rather than seeing rules as obstacles, companies can view them as guardrails that ultimately build greater trust in AI solutions, creating a stable environment for AI-driven business growth.

Corporate AI Ethics Codes

Forward-thinking companies are not waiting for laws to tell them what to do – they are proactively developing their own AI ethics codes and governance structures. In recent years, tech industry leaders especially have recognized that embedding ethics into their AI projects is both a social responsibility and a business imperative (to maintain user trust and brand reputation). This section looks at how major companies have approached AI ethics, providing models that other businesses can emulate. The trend is clear: *establishing corporate AI principles and oversight mechanisms is becoming a standard practice*, much like having a code of conduct or cybersecurity policy.

One high-profile example is Google. In 2018, after internal and public pressure (including concerns about AI being used for military purposes), Google published its set of AI Principles. Google's leadership openly acknowledged that advanced AI raises "powerful questions about its use" and that as an AI leader they have a "deep responsibility to get this right." They announced *seven principles to guide our work*, intended as "concrete standards that will actively govern our research and product development". These principles include: Be socially beneficial (i.e. AI should benefit society and contribute positively), Avoid creating or reinforcing unfair bias (strive to prevent unjust impacts especially on sensitive groups), Be built and tested for safety, Be accountable to people (meaning AI systems should have human oversight and offer explanations/appeal mechanisms), Incorporate privacy design principles, Uphold high standards of scientific excellence, and Be made available for uses that accord with these principles. In practice, Google uses these principles as a litmus test for projects – for instance, they decided not to pursue certain applications like AI for weapons or for surveillance that violate human rights. They also set up processes such as an internal review board to assess sensitive AI proposals against the principles. What's instructive for managers is that Google's principles are not just PR; they have operational bite. The company has reportedly denied or modified projects that failed ethical review. By publicizing its ethics principles, Google also invites external accountability – the public and its employees can call it out if it seems to stray from them. The lesson for businesses: Defining a clear set of AI values can guide your teams and signal to stakeholders that you're serious about responsible innovation. But it's critical to also have enforcement mechanisms (e.g. review committees, required ethics documentation for new AI products) to ensure those values truly influence decisions.

Microsoft provides another strong example with its comprehensive approach to responsible AI. Microsoft adopted Responsible AI Principles early on (around 2018) and has since operationalized them through a detailed internal standard. Microsoft's six core principles are *fairness, reliability & safety, privacy & security, inclusiveness, transparency,* and *accountability.* These mirror many of the themes we saw globally, but Microsoft turned them into an enterprise-wide program. They created an internal Office of Responsible AI and an advisory committee (at one point the Aether Committee) to oversee AI ethics across all product divisions. Importantly, Microsoft released a Responsible AI Standard – essentially a playbook that translates each principle into actionable requirements for teams (for example, for transparency they have guidelines on providing documentation and user disclosure; for fairness they require teams to conduct fairness assessments for sensitive use-cases). In 2022, Microsoft updated this Standard to version 2, making it public to share their learnings. Concrete changes that came from this effort include: Microsoft limited the use of facial recognition AI (especially features like emotion recognition which are hard to do ethically) to prevent misuse, and they implemented an AI impact assessment process that product groups must follow before launching certain AI features. They even have training modules to educate their employees on these responsible AI practices. A notable governance element is Microsoft's Responsible AI Council, a group including senior executives (with CEO Satya Nadella's support) that meets to review progress and tough cases. By integrating AI ethics at multiple levels – principles, standards, tools, and oversight bodies – Microsoft shows what a robust corporate AI ethics program can look like. The takeaway for managers is that ethical AI isn't just lofty statements; it requires institutional support. Companies should consider assigning clear ownership (an office or board) to AI ethics, adopting checklists or frameworks for product teams, and continuously updating policies as AI technology evolves. Microsoft's approach also illustrates that being open about your standards (via transparency reports or published guidelines) can enhance credibility with customers and regulators alike.

Another pioneer is IBM, a company with a long history in AI (from mainframes to IBM Watson) and a strong public stance on trust. IBM has set forth its Principles for Trust and Transparency, and notably, IBM established an internal AI Ethics Board as early as 2018. This board sits at the center of IBM's AI governance. *Its mission is to provide governance and decision-making as IBM develops, deploys, and uses AI, ensure consistency with IBM's values, and advance trustworthy AI for clients and society.* In practice, the AI Ethics Board at IBM reviews new AI research and products for ethical risks, formulates policies (like guidelines on face recognition technology), and drives education on AI ethics within the company. It sponsors various workstreams – for example, one workstream might focus on fairness in machine learning, developing bias mitigation tools, while another might engage in policy advocacy (IBM has been vocal in supporting precision regulation on AI). The Board also can assess specific use cases that raise ethical concerns, acting as an internal watchdog on high-stakes projects. IBM's approach shows that ethics must be woven into corporate DNA. They not only have top-level principles (e.g. "AI should augment humans, not replace them," "Data and insights belong to their creator," "Technology must be transparent" – all part of IBM's ethos), but also tangible structures to uphold them. IBM even appointed a Chief AI Ethics Global Leader and requires ethics training for AI developers. One highlighted decision was IBM's 2020 move to sunset its general-purpose facial recognition products, citing ethical concerns and potential for misuse in mass surveillance. IBM's CEO called for public dialogue on whether such technology should be used by government agencies – essentially putting ethics above a short-term market opportunity, which reinforced IBM's credibility on this issue.

Beyond these tech giants, many other companies have formulated AI ethics codes: Google, Microsoft, IBM were early movers, but now firms like Facebook (Meta), Salesforce, SAP, and Oracle have published AI principles. Even outside the tech sector, organizations recognize the need – for instance, banks and insurance companies (like HSBC or Allianz) are devising AI fairness charters to ensure algorithms used in lending or underwriting are fair and explainable. Corporate AI ethics codes generally cover similar ground because they're informed by the global principles we discussed. However, drafting a nice document is the easy part – the real challenge is governance. That's why the leading companies pair principles with concrete programs. It's instructive to consider a few common elements of effective corporate AI ethics programs:

- **Public AI Principles:** A written set of guidelines or values (e.g. "We will not knowingly develop AI that violates human rights") that set the tone and can be referenced in decision-making.

- **Ethics Review Process:** A workflow to vet high-risk AI projects. This might be a committee (as in Google's case for certain sensitive projects) or required checkpoints where teams must do ethical assessments and get approval before launch.

- **Training and Culture:** Internal training sessions, workshops, or even mandatory courses on AI ethics for developers and product managers. Fostering a culture where any employee can voice ethical concerns (whistleblower channels for AI issues, etc.) is key.

- **Tools and Techniques:** Companies often develop or adopt technical tools to help with responsible AI. Examples include bias detection toolkits (IBM released one as open source – AI Fairness 360), model interpretability techniques, and documentation templates like "model cards" for reporting an AI system's intended use, performance, and limitations.

- **Monitoring and Auditing:** Ongoing monitoring of AI systems in production for ethical performance. For instance, after deployment, tracking whether an AI model's decisions are drifting toward bias or if its error rates are spiking for certain groups. An internal audit function might periodically evaluate compliance with the AI principles.

- **Governance Structure:** Clear roles and accountability. This could mean having an AI Ethics Board or council (as IBM and Microsoft do) at the top, and perhaps designated ethics champions within teams. Some firms create multi-disciplinary committees including legal, technical, and business reps to tackle issues from different angles.

By establishing these elements, companies make ethics a *living practice* rather than a one-time pledge. For managers and executives reading this, the examples of Google, Microsoft, IBM, and others should be empowering. They demonstrate that it is feasible to integrate ethical considerations into business workflows without stifling innovation. In fact, these practices often spur innovation by prompting teams to find creative solutions that meet both business and ethical criteria. Moreover, having robust AI ethics governance can be a market differentiator – clients (especially enterprise and government customers) are increasingly asking vendors to demonstrate how they address AI risks. A company that can show a track record of responsible AI (with principles, processes, and an oversight structure to back it up) will stand out as a trusted provider in a data-driven world.

Frameworks for Implementation

Having principles and intentions is important, but to actually change day-to-day operations, organizations need practical frameworks to implement AI ethics. This section introduces how managers can translate high-level ideals into concrete practices using structured frameworks. Think of these as blueprints or toolkits that help embed ethical risk management throughout the AI development lifecycle. A well-known example is the NIST AI Risk Management Framework (AI RMF), released by the U.S. National Institute of Standards and Technology. While voluntary, NIST's framework provides a *systematic approach for organizations to understand and reduce the risks of AI* – essentially a recipe to ensure your AI is trustworthy and aligns with ethical principles.

The NIST AI RMF is built around four core functions: Govern, Map, Measure, and Manage. These core functions offer a *structured and practical approach to handling AI risks.* In simple terms, they correspond to the stages of risk management:

- **Govern:** Establish organizational policies and a culture for AI risk management. Governance is a cross-cutting function that means having leadership support, clear roles, and accountability for managing AI risks. For example, under "Govern," a company might create an AI ethics committee, set guidelines for procurement of AI systems, or institute training for staff. Governance sits at the center, ensuring continuous oversight and improvement of the AI risk process.

- **Map (Understand):** Contextualize and identify AI risks. In this step, teams *map* out where and how an AI system will be used, what could go wrong, and who might be impacted. It's essentially a scoping and understanding phase. For instance, before deploying an AI, you map the context: Is this AI making hiring recommendations? If so, the risks could include discrimination against protected groups, so note that. "Map" encourages thoroughly understanding the AI's purpose, the data it will use, and the societal context, which lays the groundwork for assessment.

- **Measure:** Analyze and assess the identified risks. This is the testing and metrics part – using qualitative and quantitative methods to *measure* things like fairness, accuracy, robustness of the AI system. In practice, during "Measure" you might run bias detection on your model (e.g. checking error rates for different demographic groups), evaluate explainability (can we interpret why the model gives certain outputs?), and assess security (can the model be easily fooled or attacked?). The idea is to gather evidence and metrics on how the AI system stacks up against those trustworthiness characteristics (like validity, safety, privacy, etc.).

- **Manage:** Mitigate and monitor risks based on the measurements. In this step, organizations take action on the insights gained. *Manage* involves prioritizing which risks are most significant and implementing controls or fixes. For example, if measurement found that an AI model has higher error rates for a certain group, the "Manage" step might involve retraining the model with more diverse data, or putting a human review step for those cases. Manage also means setting up ongoing monitoring – even after deployment, continue to track performance and have processes to address new issues. Essentially, "manage" is about risk treatment and continuous risk monitoring (and feeding back into governance if policies need updating).

By following the Govern-Map-Measure-Manage cycle, an organization can operationalize AI ethics in a repeatable way. It's analogous to quality management or cybersecurity frameworks that companies might already use. The NIST framework is flexible: it doesn't prescribe exact metrics or tools, but it gives a scaffold so each firm can adapt it to their context. For managers, using such a framework ensures that ethical checkpoints are not ad hoc or forgotten under pressure – they become an integrated part of project management. You can incorporate these functions into your AI project pipeline. For instance, at project kick-off, invoke the *Map* function by holding a risk brainstorming session (what could go wrong with this AI?). During model development, apply

Measure by testing the model against ethical criteria. Before deployment, apply *Manage* by fixing issues and deciding on controls (maybe limiting the use or adding user warnings if needed). And throughout, ensure *Governance* by having oversight committee sign-offs at key milestones.

Beyond NIST, there are other frameworks and resources emerging. The ISO (International Organization for Standardization) is working on an AI management system standard (ISO 42001) that will likely mirror these kinds of processes, helping organizations certify their AI governance. There are also sector-specific frameworks; for example, the healthcare AI field has guidelines for algorithmic transparency and validation (since lives are at stake with AI diagnostics). Additionally, tools like checklists, canvases, and auditing frameworks are available. One interesting practical tool is an "AI Ethics Checklist" that some companies require engineers to complete at various development stages. This might ask yes/no or short-answer questions like "Did you consider whether the training data represents all user groups?", "What's the plan to test for bias or errors?", "Is there a rollback plan if the AI causes an unexpected issue in production?". By filling such checklists, teams are prompted to think ethically and document their consideration, which governance teams can review.

One framework worth noting for implementation is the concept of AI Lifecycle accountability – ensuring ethical practices at each phase: design, development, deployment, and monitoring. Let's briefly break that down as a model managers can apply:

- **Design Phase:** Begin with ethics in mind. Incorporate diverse perspectives in brainstorming (to foresee various impacts), set clear AI objectives that align with company values, and perform an initial risk assessment (Map out potential ethical risks).

- **Development Phase:** During model building and data preparation, apply fairness and privacy techniques. Measure risks by testing model behavior on validation datasets for biases or vulnerabilities. Document all assumptions and decisions (for transparency later). Engage an internal review (governance checkpoint) if the project is high-risk.

- **Deployment Phase:** Before launching, ensure human oversight mechanisms are in place (e.g. a human will double-check the AI in critical decisions, or there's an appeals process for users). Implement transparency features (such as notifying users they are interacting with AI, as required by many guidelines and the EU Act). Conduct a final ethical compliance check – some companies have red-team exercises, trying to abuse the AI to see what happens. At deployment, clearly communicate the AI's intended use and limitations to the relevant stakeholders.

- **Monitoring Phase:** After deployment, *monitor* the AI in real-world use. Set up metrics to catch drift or emerging biases (for example, track if loan approval rates by an AI start to diverge in an odd way over time). Continuously collect feedback – both quantitative data and user/human feedback. Feed this back into model updates or policy updates. The governance body should get periodic reports. This phase ensures that AI that was ethical at launch remains so as conditions change.

Frameworks like NIST's essentially cover these ideas in a formal way. Importantly, they make AI risk management iterative and ongoing – not a one-time checkbox. The NIST core function "Govern" implies continuous learning and improvement, meaning your organization should update its risk assessments and controls as new information or tools become available.

To illustrate concretely: suppose you're a manager deploying an AI system for loan approvals. Using the framework, at Map stage you identify risk of bias against certain minorities and risk of lack of explainability to customers. At Measure stage, you test the AI on various applicant profiles and indeed find it's 5% less likely to approve equally qualified applicants from a certain ZIP code (a proxy for minority status) – a fairness issue. You also test explainability by seeing if loan officers can get a meaningful reason code from the AI's decision – if not, that's a transparency issue. Now at Manage stage, you prioritize mitigating the bias: perhaps by reweighing training data or adding a rule to override decisions in borderline cases. You also decide to use a simpler model or an explanation algorithm to generate reason codes for decisions, improving transparency. You deploy the system with these fixes and set up monitoring – e.g., every quarter you will audit a sample of decisions for bias metrics and ensure compliance with lending laws. Meanwhile, Governance is there throughout: your AI Ethics or Risk committee oversees this process, signs off that the bias was reduced to an acceptable level, and remains a point of contact for any issues that arise later (maybe a regulator inquiry or a news report – you're prepared with documentation). This example shows how a framework translates principles (like fairness, transparency) into the nuts-and-bolts of everyday AI operations.

One might ask, does this burden the business or slow down AI innovation? Initially, it does require effort – new processes, extra testing – but it is far less costly than the fallout from an unethical AI failure. Consider the cost of a lawsuit or recall if your AI is found to be discriminatory, versus the cost of an internal audit that could have caught the issue early. In fact, frameworks can spur more *innovative* thinking. Teams might discover efficiencies in the process (maybe automated bias checking tools that speed up model development by catching problems early, instead of after deployment). Also, having a risk framework in place builds confidence among stakeholders (executives, customers, regulators) that the AI can be trusted, which can accelerate approvals and adoption.

Beyond NIST, managers can also look at industry-specific frameworks or create hybrid ones. For example, the Montréal Declaration for Responsible AI provides ten principles and asks organizations to implement them – a company could map those into their own checklist. There's also the Ethics Canvas (inspired by the Business Model Canvas) that teams can fill out during design to ensure they've thought of all ethical aspects. The key is not which framework you choose, but that you choose *something* structured and adapt it to your needs.

In summary, frameworks are tools to translate high-level principles into daily practice. They prevent ethical considerations from slipping through the cracks by embedding them into project workflows. As a manager, championing a framework like the NIST AI RMF in your organization can make the difference between a reactive, firefighting approach to AI issues and a proactive, preventative approach. It gives your team a common language and process for discussing and mitigating AI risks. The result is AI systems that are not only compliant with regulations and aligned with ethical values, but also *more robust and reliable.* Responsible AI frameworks ultimately lead to better AI – ones that deliver business value *and* uphold the trust of users and society. By adopting these, managers can confidently innovate with AI, knowing they have a compass and safety net to navigate the complex landscape of AI ethics in a principled way.

Chapter 5
Tools and Techniques for Ethical AI

In previous chapters we explored the principles and challenges of ethical AI. Now we turn to practical solutions: the tools and techniques that business leaders can leverage to ensure their AI systems are fair, transparent, privacy-conscious, and well-governed. These tools empower data science teams and managers alike to implement human-centered AI, aligning algorithms with ethical standards and regulatory expectations. In this chapter, we provide a grounded look at four key areas of ethical AI practice: bias auditing and mitigation, explainability, privacy-enhancing technologies, and monitoring of AI systems. With a clear understanding of these tools and techniques, executives and managers can make principled decisions in a data-driven world, confident that their AI initiatives remain trustworthy and compliant.

Bias Auditing and Mitigation Tools

One of the first priorities in ethical AI implementation is addressing bias in models. Even well-intended AI systems can inadvertently learn unfair patterns from data, resulting in discriminatory outcomes. Bias auditing and mitigation tools help organizations detect, quantify, and reduce bias in AI models before harm occurs. A growing number of open-source toolkits are available to assist data science teams in this task, providing metrics to measure bias and algorithms to mitigate it.

Open-Source Fairness Toolkits: Notably, IBM's AI Fairness 360 (AIF360) is a comprehensive library designed to examine and mitigate bias in machine learning models. IBM's toolkit offers a full suite of fairness metrics (over 70 measurement metrics) and a range of bias mitigation algorithms developed by the research community. These algorithms span different stages of the machine learning lifecycle – from pre-processing the data (e.g. rebalancing datasets), to in-processing (adjusting the model training to penalize unfair outcomes), to post-processing (correcting model outputs after training). AIF360 even includes tutorials based on real case studies to demonstrate how to apply these bias mitigation techniques in practice. Similarly, Microsoft's Fairlearn is an open-source Python package that provides visualization dashboards and algorithms for fairness. Fairlearn's two-pronged approach lets users measure disparities in model outcomes (for example, comparing error rates or positive outcome rates across demographic groups) and then apply adjustments to address any unfair imbalances. The toolkit makes it easier for teams to see where a model might be treating groups differently and to experiment with mitigation strategies (like redistributing error rates or applying constraints so the model meets a fairness target).

How They Work: These bias auditing tools typically work by first computing bias metrics on a model. For instance, a data science team might use AIF360 or Fairlearn to calculate metrics such as *disparate impact* (the ratio of decision rates between groups), *equal opportunity difference* (difference in true positive rates between groups), or other statistical fairness measures. If the metrics reveal significant disparities – say a credit scoring model approves loans for 80% of applicants in one racial group but only 60% in another with similar creditworthiness – the toolkits then offer bias mitigation algorithms to tackle the problem. Some algorithms modify the training data (a pre-processing approach) by reweighting or resampling data to balance representations. Other methods adjust the model training process itself (in-processing), for example by adding fairness constraints or modifying the model's objective function to penalize biased mistakes. Yet other methods operate on the predictions after the model is trained (post-processing), by shifting decision thresholds or relabeling certain outputs to close the fairness gaps. An important insight is that there is no one-size-fits-all solution – each approach involves trade-offs, and these toolkits allow teams to try different techniques and evaluate the results.

Real-World Scenario – Auditing a Credit Model: To illustrate how managers might deploy these tools, consider a bank auditing its AI credit scoring model for racial bias. The bank's data science team can use IBM AIF360 to analyze the model's loan approval rates for different racial groups. Suppose they find that the model's approval rate for minority applicants is notably lower than for white applicants with similar financial profiles – a red flag for potential bias. Using the toolkit, they compute fairness metrics which confirm a disparate impact below the acceptable threshold. The team then selects a bias mitigation algorithm from AIF360's library – for example, a reweighting algorithm that adjusts the training dataset so that minority applicants are given slightly higher weight during model training. After retraining the model with this technique, they find the disparity in approval rates has narrowed, improving fairness without drastically hurting overall accuracy. They document these results and can present to management: the bias issue was identified and proactively addressed using a proven tool. This kind of hands-on bias audit and mitigation process is increasingly considered a best practice, especially in sensitive applications like lending, hiring, or insurance. Managers don't need to be data scientists to champion it; they can ensure their teams have integrated such bias checks into model development, much like software testing is integrated into product development.

Other Tools in the Ecosystem: In addition to IBM's and Microsoft's offerings, there are other notable tools worth mentioning. Aequitas, developed by researchers at the University of Chicago, is an open-source fairness audit toolkit aimed at both technical and non-technical stakeholders. It produces easy-to-understand reports on potential bias and is designed to be used by policymakers or risk officers who need to evaluate models without delving into code. There are also proprietary solutions emerging for enterprise needs. For example, PricewaterhouseCoopers' AI Bias Analyzer provides a web-based bias detection platform with dashboards and built-in bias mitigation recommendations. Startups like Fiddler AI offer AI observability platforms that combine bias detection, drift monitoring, and explainability in one interface. The proliferation of these tools sends a clear message: businesses now have ample means to conduct bias "health checks" on AI models. Forward-looking companies are integrating bias audits as a routine step in model development and deployment. By using bias mitigation toolkits, they not only reduce ethical and legal risks, but also build more robust models – often improving model performance for under-served segments and ensuring decisions are based on merit rather than flawed correlations.

In summary, bias auditing tools give managers tangible control over AI fairness. Rather than guessing or simply trusting that teams will be fair, executives can mandate the use of these toolkits and request bias reports for high-stakes AI systems. The result is AI that aligns better with corporate values of non-discrimination and inclusivity, transforming ethical principles into measurable outcomes.

Explainability and Interpretability Techniques

Even when an AI model is made fairer, it can still be a "black box" – inscrutable in how it reaches its decisions. For business leaders, explainability is crucial: it builds trust, satisfies regulators, and helps ensure the AI is doing what it's supposed to do. This section discusses techniques to make AI decisions more transparent and understandable, from using inherently interpretable models to employing advanced explainability tools for complex algorithms. We also highlight emerging best practices like model cards, which document model behavior for all stakeholders. The overarching trend is that explaining AI is no longer optional; customers, regulators, and business partners increasingly expect clear answers to the question, "Why did the AI do that?"

Inherently Interpretable Models: The simplest route to AI transparency is using models that are understandable by design. Traditional statistical models such as linear regression or logistic regression, and machine learning models like decision trees or simple rule-based systems, have the advantage of producing explanations that humans can follow. For example, a decision tree might approve a loan because *income > $50,000 and debt-to-income ratio < 40%* – a logic that a manager or customer can readily comprehend. Similarly, a score from a logistic regression can be broken down by feature contributions (e.g. pointing out how age, income, and credit score contributed to a creditworthiness score). These inherently interpretable models are often suitable for less complex decisions or when transparency is paramount. In fact, some highly regulated industries (like healthcare or finance) may favor a slightly less accurate but interpretable model over a more accurate black-box model for certain decisions, just so they can justify outcomes to regulators and consumers. Managers should be aware of this trade-off: sometimes simplicity aids accountability.

Post-hoc Explanation Methods (LIME, SHAP, etc.): In many cases, however, businesses will leverage more complex AI techniques – ensemble methods, gradient-boosted machines, or deep neural networks – because of their superior accuracy or capabilities. To unlock transparency from these black-box models, data scientists use post-hoc explainability tools. Two widely-used techniques are LIME (Local Interpretable Model-agnostic Explanations) and SHAP (SHapley Additive Explanations).

- **LIME** works by perturbing inputs and observing changes in the model's predictions to learn which features are most influential for a specific prediction. For instance, if an AI model predicts a certain customer will churn (leave a service), LIME might reveal that the number of recent support tickets and months since last login were the top factors driving that prediction. LIME essentially builds a simple, linear approximation of the model's behavior in the vicinity of one prediction, producing a list of features with weights – a straightforward "reason code" for the decision.

- **SHAP** is another powerful technique based on cooperative game theory (Shapley values). SHAP values attribute an importance value to each feature for a given prediction, showing how each feature moves the prediction above or below the average expectation. One advantage of SHAP is that its explanations satisfy certain desirable properties (like consistency) and it provides both local explanations (for one prediction) and global insight (aggregate feature importance). For example, a SHAP analysis on a complex insurance risk model might show that for a particular applicant, owning a sports car added +5 points to their risk score, while having no prior accidents subtracted -3 points. Summing all such contributions explains why the model gave the final prediction. In one real-world case, an auto insurance company used SHAP on its AI model and discovered that certain combinations of vehicle type and driver age were associated with much higher risk. This insight, surfaced by an explainability tool, allowed them to adjust their model and underwriting policies, ultimately improving performance and fairness.

Model Cards for Transparency: Beyond explaining individual predictions, organizations are adopting model documentation practices to provide transparency at a higher level. Model cards are a recently introduced concept (first proposed by researchers at Google in 2018) – essentially, a short report accompanying a machine learning model that details its intended use, performance, and limitations. A typical model card might include information such as: what data was the model trained on; how well does it perform overall and for different subgroups; what assumptions or ethical considerations were noted (e.g., the model should not be used for decisions beyond a certain context); and who to contact for questions about the model. This is akin to a nutrition label, but for an AI model's ethical and performance characteristics. Leading companies are increasingly publishing model cards especially for high-profile AI systems. For example, when Meta and Microsoft released their Llama 2 large language model, they provided an extensive model card listing the model's training data, evaluation results, and even its environmental impact (energy usage), as well as ethical considerations and limitations. For managers, model cards are useful tools to communicate with stakeholders – including customers, auditors, and regulators – about what an AI system is and isn't intended to do. If a client or regulator asks, "Can you explain how your AI works and whether it's been tested for bias?", the model card serves as a ready-made reference detailing those points in clear language.

Regulatory and Customer Expectations: It's important for business leaders to recognize that explainability is not just an internal concern – it's becoming an external requirement. Customers are more likely to trust and adopt AI-driven services if they can get understandable reasons for decisions. In domains like finance, customers denied a loan by an algorithm will ask for justification, and indeed laws in many jurisdictions require providing key factors for adverse decisions (for instance, the U.S. Equal Credit Opportunity Act mandates that lenders give applicants reasons for denial, even if an AI made the decision). Regulators, too, are sharpening their focus. A recent example from the insurance industry: the California Department of Insurance issued a bulletin in 2022 requiring that insurance companies must be able to explain any adverse actions (like raising a premium or denying a claim) that are based on complex algorithms. In Europe, the forthcoming EU AI Act includes provisions around transparency and the "right to an explanation" for high-risk AI systems. Even when not explicitly mandated, explaining AI decisions is key to proving compliance with anti-discrimination laws and to avoiding reputational damage. As a McKinsey analysis noted, *customers, regulators, and the public at large need confidence that AI models are making decisions in an accurate and fair way* – and providing explanations is central to building that confidence.

Implementing Explainability in Practice: To meet these expectations, companies are building explainability into their AI governance processes. MLOps (Machine Learning Operations) teams now often include explainability checks as part of model deployment pipelines. For instance, before a new predictive model is rolled out, the team might generate a report of the top features influencing the model and have domain experts or compliance officers review whether those drivers make business sense and don't reflect any inadvertent bias. Tools like LIME and SHAP can be integrated such that whenever the model makes an especially high-stakes decision (say, declining a loan or flagging a transaction as fraud), an explanation is automatically logged or provided to the user. Business executives, even if they are not deep in the technical details, should encourage a culture where no significant AI decision goes unexplained. By demanding that their teams can always answer "why did the AI do that?", leaders ensure that the AI remains aligned with the organization's values and can be defended under scrutiny. In summary, explainability techniques turn AI from an inscrutable wizard into a transparent advisor – something much easier to trust and hold accountable.

Privacy-Enhancing Technologies

As companies gather and leverage more data for AI, concerns around privacy and data protection have come to the forefront. Business leaders must balance the hunger for insights with the obligation to respect customer privacy and comply with data protection laws. Fortunately, a suite of privacy-enhancing technologies (PETs) has emerged to allow AI models to learn from data without exposing sensitive information. This section covers key PETs – including differential privacy, federated learning, and strong encryption – and explains how they help organizations extract value from data while safeguarding individual privacy. By adopting these technologies, businesses can build AI solutions that are both innovative and trustworthy, avoiding the pitfalls of data misuse or breaches.

Differential Privacy: One powerful approach to protecting privacy is known as differential privacy, which involves injecting carefully calibrated randomness (noise) into data or query results so that individual entries become indistinguishable in the aggregate analysis. In simpler terms, differential privacy is "the statistical science of trying to learn as much as possible about a group while learning as little as possible about any individual in it". When a company applies differential privacy, it can still derive useful patterns from large datasets – for example, average spending habits of customers, or the most common routes drivers take in a city – but it mathematically ensures that nothing specific can be learned about any single person. Tech companies have been pioneers in using differential privacy. Apple, for instance, has used differential privacy in iOS to collect usage statistics (like the most typed new words on the keyboard) to improve auto-correct features, without ever storing exact user keystrokes. The data sent back is perturbed with noise so that Apple can see general trends but *not* reconstruct a particular user's typing. Likewise, the U.S. Census Bureau applied differential privacy in the 2020 Census data release, to protect the identities of respondents while still providing useful demographic statistics – a landmark use of this technique in the public sector. For businesses, leveraging differential privacy can mean incorporating tools or algorithms that aggregate data with privacy guarantees. For example, an e-commerce firm could use a differential privacy tool to analyze customer behavior across millions of records to personalize offerings, in a way that prevents any single customer's behavior from being singled out. This not only helps comply with privacy regulations (like GDPR, which emphasizes data minimization and protection) but also builds customer trust: people are more willing to share data if they know it's handled in a privacy-preserving way. Differential privacy essentially offers a win-win: deep insights *and* respect for individual privacy.

Federated Learning: Another breakthrough in privacy-preserving AI is federated learning. Traditional machine learning involves centralizing all data on a server to train a model, which raises concerns when data is sensitive (medical records, personal texts, etc.) and cannot be easily shared. Federated learning flips the script by bringing the model to the data instead of bringing data to the model. In a federated learning setup, the AI model is sent out to devices or servers where data resides (e.g., users' smartphones, or different hospital databases). The model is trained locally on each dataset, and only the learned parameters or gradients are sent back to a central server, where they are aggregated to form a global model. Crucially, the raw data never leaves its original location. A classic example is how Google uses federated learning for the Gboard smartphone keyboard: the system learns to improve text predictions by training on the typing data stored on each user's phone, and Google's servers only receive the model updates (which are essentially mathematical weights) rather than any individual's keystrokes or messages. This way, your phone contributes to a better predictive text model for everyone without sharing your personal messages. Federated learning is increasingly being used in other domains such as healthcare (allowing multiple hospitals to collaboratively train AI models on patient data without sharing that data with each other), finance (different banks training a joint fraud detection model without exposing customer records), and more. The benefits are multifold: it addresses privacy and data residency concerns, reduces the risk of large-scale data breaches (since data isn't pooled centrally), and can even reduce latency (since models can run locally for personalization). Business leaders should take note that federated learning enables cooperation across data silos – you might partner with other institutions in your industry to build better AI models together, all while each of you keeps your proprietary data secure. Adopting federated approaches can thus drive innovation that would be impossible if everyone guarded their data in isolation due to privacy constraints.

Encryption and Secure Data Handling: While differential privacy and federated learning are relatively new techniques born out of the AI era, tried-and-true methods like strong encryption remain fundamental for ethical AI. Encryption should be applied to data at rest (in databases or storage) and in transit (moving over networks) such that even if data is intercepted or accessed by unauthorized parties, it remains unintelligible. Modern encryption standards (like AES-256 for data storage, TLS for data in transit) are extremely robust when properly implemented. Managers should ensure that their AI systems and data pipelines employ encryption by default – for instance, if an AI model is trained on customer data stored in the cloud, those storage buckets should be encrypted, and any communication between the training environment and the storage should be over encrypted channels. Beyond basic encryption, advanced cryptographic techniques are emerging to enable new capabilities: one example is homomorphic encryption, which allows computations on encrypted data without decrypting it. Although homomorphic encryption is computationally heavy and not yet widely used in commercial applications, it holds promise for scenarios where even the model host shouldn't see the raw data (imagine an AI cloud service that can make predictions on encrypted client data without ever decrypting it – providing maximal privacy). Another technique is secure multi-party computation (SMPC), which allows multiple parties to jointly compute a function over their inputs (like training a model) without any party having to reveal their own data to the others. These techniques are still maturing, but they signal where the industry is headed: toward privacy-by-design AI, where from the ground up the algorithms are built to respect data confidentiality.

Data Governance and Compliance: Privacy-enhancing technologies are most effective when coupled with strong data governance frameworks. This means having policies and processes in place to manage data responsibly throughout its lifecycle – from collection and consent, to storage, access control, and eventual deletion. Business executives should champion a culture of privacy where any AI project begins with questions like: *Do we really need this data? Have we obtained it ethically and with permission? How do we limit access and ensure compliance with laws?* For example, adopting a framework like the NIST Privacy Framework or ISO standards can provide guidelines to align AI development with privacy principles. Good data governance also involves regular audits of data practices, training employees on data ethics, and keeping abreast of privacy regulations (GDPR, California Consumer Privacy Act, etc.). By using privacy-enhancing tech under the umbrella of robust governance, companies can innovate with data while staying on the right side of both the law and public opinion.

To illustrate the payoff: consider a scenario in healthcare. A hospital network wants to use AI to improve patient outcomes by analyzing data from all its clinics. Instead of pooling all patient data in one place (which could violate patient consent agreements and raise breach risks), they implement federated learning to train a model across hospitals. They add differential privacy so that any reported insights have noise added to mask individuals. All data transfers are encrypted. They also ensure only authorized personnel and systems can trigger these analyses, per their governance policy. The result is a powerful predictive model that might, say, help detect early signs of disease across a large population – achieved without compromising patient privacy. Business leaders who invest in such privacy-enhancing approaches send a message to customers and regulators: *we value data privacy as much as data profit*. This not only prevents costly violations but also builds a reputation for integrity in a data-driven world.

Monitoring and Auditing AI Systems

Deploying an AI system is not the end of a company's ethical responsibilities – in fact, it's just the beginning of a new phase. Over time, AI models can drift, performance can degrade, or unanticipated behaviors might emerge as conditions change. Continuous monitoring and auditing of AI systems is therefore essential to maintain their integrity and fairness. This section provides guidance on setting up ongoing oversight for AI in production, from automated monitoring dashboards to periodic audits and check-ups. With the right processes and tools in place (including emerging AI governance software), managers can confidently keep AI systems on track without having to micromanage each algorithm's every move.

The Need for Ongoing Oversight: AI models learn from data – and if the world represented by that data changes, models can start making errors or even unfair decisions. This phenomenon, known as model drift, comes in a few forms. *Data drift* means the input data distributions shift (for example, a retail model trained on last year's sales data may become less accurate if consumer preferences change this year). *Concept drift* means the relationship between inputs and outcomes changes (for example, if an economic downturn alters what factors signal credit risk, a previously sound lending model might start failing to predict defaults accurately). Additionally, AI systems might encounter edge cases or unforeseen scenarios in operation that weren't in the training data, leading to unexpected outputs. Continuous monitoring is about catching these issues early. Just as financial controllers monitor transactions for anomalies or security teams monitor networks for intrusions, AI teams should monitor models for signs of trouble – whether it's a drop in accuracy, an uptick in bias, or other anomalies in usage.

Automated Monitoring Tools: Fortunately, we don't have to monitor AI systems manually; there are tools that specialize in this. Many MLOps and AI governance platforms provide dashboards that track key metrics of deployed models. For example, IBM has developed an AI governance offering (part of its watsonx suite) that includes automated monitoring of metrics like fairness, drift, and performance throughout a model's lifecycle. IBM's Watson OpenScale is a tool that continuously evaluates predictive models on metrics such as accuracy and fairness, and it can even flag bias in real time by comparing outcomes across groups. If a deviation is detected – say the model's error rate for a certain demographic has increased beyond a set threshold – the system can alert stakeholders or even trigger mitigating actions. OpenScale also monitors model drift by tracking changes in input data statistics and can send an alert if the data the model is seeing in production starts to differ significantly from the training data distribution. Similarly, other enterprise platforms like Fiddler AI and TruEra (mentioned earlier) integrate monitoring: they provide a view of model performance over time, drift detection, and even *what-if analysis* tools to simulate how changes in data might affect outcomes. These tools essentially act as an AI dashboard for managers, summarizing the health of AI systems in operation. A manager could glance at a report showing, for instance, that "Model X's accuracy has been stable at 90% with no significant bias drift in the last quarter, and all monitored fairness metrics are within approved range." This gives confidence that the AI is behaving as expected – or conversely, it might show where attention is needed.

Periodic Audits and Model Check-ups: In addition to real-time monitoring, companies are instituting regular AI audits. An AI audit might be conducted quarterly or biannually, involving a thorough review of a model's performance, fairness, security, and compliance with any new regulations. Think of it as a scheduled maintenance for algorithms. For example, a bank might convene a review of its credit scoring AI every six months to re-evaluate its fairness metrics on the latest data, check if any new data privacy laws affect its input data, and ensure the model hasn't been surpassed by a newer technique that would warrant an update. These audits can involve multidisciplinary teams – data scientists, business process owners, compliance officers, and even external auditors or ethicists in some cases – to provide a 360-degree evaluation. Some organizations even create "AI audit trails" using tools that log every decision the AI makes along with the context, so that any questionable decision can be traced and examined after the fact. The key message for managers is that an ethical AI program requires ongoing vigilance: launching a "fair" model is not a permanent guarantee, so one must keep checking and tuning.

AI Governance Software: To support this continuous oversight, major tech companies are rolling out governance software that automates many governance tasks. We mentioned IBM's watsonx.governance – within that, AI Factsheets automatically document each model's history and metrics, and OpenPages handles risk and compliance workflows. These kinds of tools help track, for instance, whether a model has received the necessary approvals before deployment, whether it has been retrained on schedule, and whether it's currently under any alerts for issues. They can serve as a centralized system of record for AI models, much like a CRM is for customers or an ERP is for resource planning. By adopting such tools, companies can scale up their AI usage without losing oversight. It's not hard to imagine in the near future an executive dashboard that lists all the AI models in production across an enterprise, with green/yellow/red indicators for their ethical and operational status (green means all good, yellow might mean e.g. "data drift detected – retraining recommended", red could mean "model paused due to bias alert"). In fact, IBM's governance platform already allows setting preset thresholds and policies – for example, if a fairness metric goes below a certain level, it could automatically trigger retraining or send notifications.

Encouraging a Proactive Culture: The tone around monitoring is ultimately *encouraging*. Managers should not view these tools as burdensome controls, but rather as safety nets that enable more confident deployment of AI. When you know that an AI system is being closely watched by an automated monitoring service and will raise a flag if something goes awry, you can afford to rely on it more in daily operations. It also means you don't have to second-guess every decision the AI makes – the system will surface issues for your attention. This avoids the scenario of "holding the AI's hand" constantly; instead, you establish the rules and let the monitoring framework enforce them. With periodic audits, you also instill a discipline of continuous improvement – teams will prepare for the fact that their models must "pass the test" every so often, leading them to maintain and improve models proactively.

Finally, continuous monitoring and audits demonstrate accountability to external stakeholders. If a regulator inquires how your company ensures an AI hasn't become biased over time, you can point to your live fairness dashboards or audit logs as evidence of governance. If customers wonder how you maintain quality in AI-driven services, you can share that you have real-time performance monitors and routine audits just as you would for human-driven processes. In sum, monitoring and auditing tools allow companies to reap the benefits of AI at scale without falling asleep at the wheel. They operationalize the principle that ethical AI is not a one-off achievement but an ongoing commitment. Armed with these oversight techniques, business leaders can confidently steer their AI initiatives, knowing that if something starts to go off-course, they will be the first to know and can take action swiftly.

Chapter Summary: In this chapter, we covered the practical side of implementing ethical AI in business. We saw that bias auditing and mitigation tools like IBM AIF360 and Microsoft Fairlearn give teams the ability to measure and reduce unfairness in models, ensuring decisions are equitable. We explored explainability techniques – from using interpretable models to deploying LIME/SHAP and creating model cards – which together help answer the critical "why" behind AI decisions and build trust with users and regulators. We discussed privacy-enhancing technologies such as differential privacy and federated learning that enable innovation with data while fiercely protecting individual privacy, a must for compliance and public confidence. Lastly, we underscored the importance of monitoring and auditing AI systems post-deployment, leveraging tools that track fairness, accuracy, and drift so that AI remains reliable and principled over time.

The common thread is that there are now concrete tools and methodologies to translate ethical AI principles into day-to-day practice. Business executives and managers do not have to simply hope their AI is ethical – they can actively verify and enforce it using the techniques described. By investing in these tools and fostering a culture that values ethical oversight, organizations can make AI a force for good in a data-driven world, harnessing its benefits while managing its risks. The path to human-centered AI is clear: equip your teams with the right tools, stay informed of the model's behavior, and always be ready to explain and justify your AI's actions. In doing so, you ensure that technology serves your business goals *and* upholds the values that define your brand.

Chapter 6

Ethics in Action – Real-World Case Studies

In this chapter, we explore four pivotal real-world case studies where ethical challenges in AI became strikingly clear. Each case illustrates how well-intentioned algorithms can go awry and what lessons managers can draw about implementing AI responsibly. We examine what happened, why it happened, and the key takeaways — from biased hiring software to credit discrimination, a massive data privacy scandal, and a bold corporate stance on facial recognition. The tone is grounded and informational, showing that ethical principles in technology are not abstract ideals but practical necessities for businesses in a data-driven world.

Biased Hiring Algorithm at Amazon

Amazon's experiment with an AI-driven hiring tool serves as a cautionary tale about unintended bias in machine learning. In the mid-2010s, Amazon developed a résumé screening algorithm intended to streamline recruitment by automatically identifying top talent. The goal was ambitious: feed the system hundreds of past resumes and have it learn to rank candidates from one to five stars, similar to product ratings. However, within a year of deployment, the company discovered a serious flaw – the AI was not gender-neutral. In fact, the model was systematically favoring male candidates and penalizing resumes that indicated the applicant was a woman.

What went wrong technically? The root cause was traced to the training data and the patterns the AI learned. Amazon's model had been trained on 10 years of the company's own hiring data, a period during which the tech industry (and Amazon's workforce) was overwhelmingly male. Essentially, the AI observed who had been hired and successful in the past and assumed those patterns equated to the best candidates. Male candidates and male-associated terms dominated the historical data, so the algorithm "taught itself" that male applicants were preferable. It began penalizing resumes that included the word "women's," such as references to "women's chess club captain," and it even downgraded graduates of all-women's colleges. In other words, the AI incorporated the existing gender bias in the dataset into its model of an ideal candidate.

This technical blind spot — learning from biased historical data without context — led to tangible discriminatory behavior. According to reports, about 60% of the candidates the tool selected were male, far above a balanced rate. Amazon's developers tried to correct the most obvious biases by editing the program to ignore explicit gendered terms, but they realized this was not a guarantee of fairness. The AI could easily find other proxies or patterns that correlated with gender (or other biases) without using the banned keywords. For example, if women had less frequent certain jargon or style of phrasing on their resumes due to systemic factors, the AI might still favor the male patterns.

Within a year of testing, Amazon recognized the tool's limitations and decided to shut it down entirely. Executives lost confidence that the AI could be made truly fair, and they did not want to rely on a system with discriminatory tendencies. Notably, Amazon stated that the experimental tool was never used as the sole arbiter of hiring decisions — recruiters looked at its recommendations but did not blindly follow them. Still, the company understood that even assisting in hiring with a biased algorithm could reinforce inequity, so they discontinued the project. This early ending underscores an important point: sometimes the most responsible action is to pull the plug on an AI system that proves biased or unreliable rather than pushing forward and potentially harming real applicants.

Blind spots in development: Amazon's team was comprised of skilled technologists, yet they missed critical ethical considerations in development. One blind spot was homogeneity in training data – they used past hiring data without ensuring diversity in those examples. If the past was biased, the AI simply learned that bias. Another blind spot was the lack of bias testing upfront. It appears the team discovered the gender bias only after deployment, when outcomes made the disparity obvious. Had they proactively audited the model's recommendations for demographic patterns before using it, they might have caught the issue earlier or adjusted the approach (for instance, by supplementing the training data with more gender-balanced examples or explicitly instructing the model to ignore gendered cues). Additionally, the focus on technical performance (like matching resumes to past hiring decisions) may have overshadowed considerations of fairness. The developers were seeking a "holy grail" of recruitment efficiency, but in doing so they overlooked how the algorithm made its choices. This underscores how important human oversight and diverse perspectives are when building AI for sensitive functions like hiring.

Lessons learned: Amazon's experience taught the tech industry a valuable lesson about AI fairness. The case demonstrated that algorithms are only as unbiased as the data we feed them. If historical data reflects societal biases (here, a gender imbalance in tech hiring), an unguided AI will likely propagate or even amplify those biases. It highlighted the necessity of diverse training data – including data that represent the groups you want to be treated fairly – and the need for continuous bias testing and monitoring. Amazon's tool also illustrates the risks of treating AI as a magical solution for complex human decisions like hiring. As one Carnegie Mellon AI expert noted, ensuring algorithms are fair, interpretable, and explainable is still a far-off challenge. In absence of those assurances, companies must be cautious.

- *Key Takeaways (Amazon Hiring Algorithm):*

    o **Bias can be inherited from data:** AI models can learn discriminatory patterns if trained on biased historical data. Regular audits of training data and model outputs are essential to spot such bias early.

    o **Human oversight is critical:** Automated tools should not operate unchecked in hiring or other high-stakes decisions. Amazon's recruiters did not fully trust the AI and kept humans in the loop – a prudent approach given the circumstances.

- o **Stop or fix flawed AI:** If an AI system is found to be biased or unreliable, disabling or reworking it is often the most ethical choice. Amazon's decision to shut down the biased system after a short trial period shows a willingness to prioritize fairness over efficiency.

- o **Diversity in design teams and data:** This case underlines the importance of having diverse teams develop AI (to foresee bias issues) and using diverse datasets. A broader range of perspectives might have anticipated that an all-male training history would skew the results.

Gender Bias in Credit Decisions (Apple Card)

When Apple launched its highly anticipated Apple Card in 2019, it promised a new level of simplicity and innovation in personal finance. But soon after its release, the Apple Card became embroiled in a controversy over alleged gender bias in credit limits. The card, issued by Goldman Sachs, was advertised as using a "algorithmic credit decision" system to determine each user's credit line. By late 2019, several tech entrepreneurs and Apple customers noticed a troubling pattern: Women were receiving far lower credit limits than men with similar (or even weaker) financial profiles. The spark came from a series of public tweets, notably by David Heinemeier Hansson (creator of Ruby on Rails) and Apple's own co-founder Steve Wozniak, who compared their credit limits with those of their wives. In one widely shared example, Hansson was given 20 times the credit limit of his wife, despite the fact that they file joint tax returns and his wife actually had a higher credit score. Wozniak added that he experienced a 10x credit limit disparity compared to his wife, even though they shared all assets and accounts. These personal anecdotes suggested a systemic issue: the algorithm appeared to be assigning significantly lower credit ceilings to female applicants.

The public outcry on social media quickly caught the attention of regulators. New York's Department of Financial Services (DFS) announced an official inquiry into Goldman Sachs' credit card practices within days of the viral tweets. The incident raised an uncomfortable question: How could an algorithm that presumably did not *explicitly* consider gender still produce such apparently gender-skewed outcomes? Goldman Sachs, for its part, denied any overt discrimination. A spokesman stated that their credit decisions were based solely on creditworthiness factors like income, credit scores, and debt, and "not on factors like gender, race, age, sexual orientation or any other basis prohibited by law". In other words, the bank insisted the algorithm was *gender-blind* by design. Yet, the evidence of disparate impact was hard to ignore, suggesting that the algorithm might be using other inputs that act as proxies for gender. For example, if women on average had shorter credit histories (perhaps due to systemic economic factors or differing financial behaviors), the model might unintentionally treat that as a risk factor, resulting in lower limits. Other potential proxies could include the types of purchases, patterns in spending, or even the fact that a married couple's finances were evaluated individually rather than jointly, which could disadvantage a spouse who, say, has fewer accounts in their name.

As the DFS investigation got underway, the regulator made it clear that "unintentional" bias is no excuse. In a public statement, New York's financial regulator emphasized, *"Any algorithm that intentionally or not results in discriminatory treatment of women or any other protected class violates New York law."* This is a crucial point: even if Goldman's algorithm did not consider gender as an input, the outcome of granting women dramatically lower credit constituted a discriminatory effect. Such "disparate impact" is unlawful in lending. The implication for businesses using AI is profound — companies are responsible for the outcomes of their algorithms, not just their intentions. In this case, the DFS investigation likely examined whether factors used in the credit model (like income, credit utilization, etc.) correlated with gender in a way that produced bias. It also examined the development and testing process Goldman Sachs used: did they test for gender bias before launch? Could they explain how the model computes credit limits?

The Apple Card controversy is a textbook example of how algorithmic bias can lead to public relations crises and legal scrutiny. Here was a flagship Apple product (with a major bank behind it) being slammed by some of the very tech-savvy consumers it targeted. The fact that Steve Wozniak – an Apple icon – spoke out gave the story additional traction. The media dubbed the algorithm "sexist", and the incident became headline news in technology and business press. Beyond the immediate reputational damage to Apple and Goldman Sachs, the episode sparked a broader conversation: How many other financial algorithms might be quietly perpetuating bias? It also highlighted the black box nature of AI in finance – consumers found it difficult to get clear answers or human intervention ("Hard to get to a human for a correction," Wozniak lamented). This lack of transparency further fueled frustration.

In response to the outcry, Goldman Sachs eventually agreed to re-review credit limits for affected customers and cooperate with regulators. The company did not publicly disclose the inner workings of its algorithm, citing proprietary technology, but it faced immense pressure to ensure such disparities would not happen moving forward. For managers and organizations, the Apple Card case underscores the importance of fairness testing and transparency when deploying AI in customer-facing decisions. Had Goldman Sachs performed extensive bias analysis on the model (for example, simulating outcomes for men vs. women with identical profiles), they might have caught this issue before launch. The case also suggests that when bias concerns are raised, companies should respond swiftly with investigation and remediation, rather than defensively insisting the algorithm is infallible.

- *Key Takeaways (Apple Card and Algorithmic Bias):*
  - **Proxies can perpetuate bias:** Even if an algorithm isn't deliberately using a sensitive attribute like gender, it may inadvertently use correlated data (proxies) that produce a biased outcome. In credit decisions, factors that seem

neutral can still skew against a group if not carefully checked.

o **Disparate impact is unacceptable:** The Apple Card incident reinforces that results matter. Under law and ethics, it's not enough that an AI is designed to be neutral — if the effect is discriminatory, the company is accountable. Businesses must evaluate their AI's impact on different demographics and be prepared to explain and correct any inequities.

o **The cost of bias is high:** This single algorithmic issue led to a regulatory investigation, negative headlines worldwide, and loss of consumer trust for Apple and Goldman Sachs. The PR fallout shows how brand reputation can be damaged by AI missteps. For managers, it's a reminder that ethical lapses in AI aren't hidden in a back office — they can become front-page news.

o **Implement human oversight and appeals:** Customers should have a clear, accessible way to get human review of algorithmic decisions. In lending, regulators expect that consumers can ask for reconsideration. A lack of human oversight not only frustrates users (as Wozniak noted) but also increases legal risks.

o **Regular audits and diverse testing:** Before and after deployment, algorithms should be tested with diverse scenarios (different genders, ages, ethnic backgrounds, etc. where applicable) to detect bias. Including women and minority experts in the development and testing process can help identify bias that homogeneous teams might miss.

Data Privacy Scandal – Facebook and Cambridge Analytica

Perhaps one of the most infamous cases in digital ethics is the Facebook–Cambridge Analytica data scandal. This episode, which came to light in 2018, vividly demonstrates how mishandling user data can not only violate privacy but also undermine democratic processes and incur enormous regulatory penalties. The case revolves around Cambridge Analytica, a British political consulting firm, and its exploitation of Facebook user data. In the mid-2010s, Cambridge Analytica obtained personal data from Facebook on tens of millions of users without their consent, then used that data to craft targeted political advertisements and strategies. The scandal's scope was massive — it was eventually revealed that the profiles of over 50 million Facebook users were harvested without permission in what was one of the largest data breaches in Facebook's history.

The data was collected via a seemingly innocuous personality quiz app developed by an academic, which only a few hundred thousand Facebook users installed. However, due to Facebook's Open Graph API policies at the time, the app was allowed to gather data not just from the people who took the quiz, but also from all their friends. This exponential access meant that from a few hundred thousand direct users, data on tens of millions of their friends was scooped up. Facebook's terms prohibited selling or misusing this data, but Cambridge Analytica, in partnership with the app's creator, violated those terms by acquiring and retaining the data for political microtargeting. Cambridge Analytica's goal was to use the data to influence elections – notably, they provided analytics and support to Ted Cruz's 2016 U.S. presidential primary campaign and later to Donald Trump's presidential campaign. By analyzing Facebook "likes," connections, and other personal information, the firm built psychographic profiles to predict and potentially sway voters' behavior.

When a whistleblower (Christopher Wylie, a former Cambridge Analytica employee) exposed the extent of this data harvesting to the press in March 2018, the news ignited global outrage. It was a watershed moment for public awareness of digital privacy. Users felt betrayed that Facebook had allowed their personal information to be misused on such a scale. The public's trust in Facebook plummeted. A survey by the Ponemon Institute found that in the immediate aftermath, only 27% of Americans believed Facebook would protect their personal data, down from 79% the year before – a spectacular collapse in confidence. The hashtag #DeleteFacebook trended as users voiced their anger. Facebook's stock price even took a hit, losing as much as $100 billion in market value in the days after the revelations. These reactions underscore how digital ethics failures can translate into tangible business consequences – loss of user engagement, damage to brand, and financial repercussions.

From an ethical and managerial standpoint, what went wrong at Facebook? Several issues emerged:

- **Lack of oversight and due diligence:** Facebook did not adequately vet how third-party developers were using its data. Once the data left Facebook's hands (via the app's access), there was little monitoring. It wasn't until two years after the data was initially harvested (and after press inquiries) that Facebook took action to suspend Cambridge Analytica from the platform. Internal emails later showed Facebook knew of the improper data sharing earlier but failed to alert users or ensure deletion of the data.

- **No informed consent:** Users whose data was taken had no idea this was happening. They had never consented to have their information used for political campaigning. The friends of the quiz-takers, in particular, had not even used the app. This violates a core principle of data ethics: people should have control over how their personal data is used. In this case, Facebook's policies were so loose that they allowed a major consent breach.

- **Data turned into a weapon:** Cambridge Analytica effectively weaponized personal data against the people it was taken from, by using it to manipulate voter sentiment ("to target their inner demons," as Wylie described it). This crossed an ethical line, showing how data analytics can be misused in ways companies and regulators did not anticipate. It wasn't just a privacy violation;

it became a societal and political issue, undermining trust in social media's role in democracy.

The fallout for Facebook was severe. Besides the public backlash, it faced multiple government investigations. In the United States, the Federal Trade Commission (FTC) launched a probe into whether Facebook's handling of data violated a 2012 consent decree that required Facebook to safeguard user privacy. The result was a record-breaking $5 billion fine levied by the FTC in 2019 – the largest privacy-related fine in U.S. history at that time. In the UK, Facebook paid a smaller fine (£500,000, the maximum allowed under old UK data laws) for violating data protection principles. Moreover, Facebook had to implement new compliance measures, and its CEO Mark Zuckerberg was called to testify before the U.S. Congress and EU Parliament, facing tough questions about the company's commitment to ethics and privacy.

For managers, the Cambridge Analytica scandal is a stark reminder of the importance of digital ethics and data governance. Had Facebook leadership and product managers been more proactive in enforcing data-sharing policies and auditing third-party developers, this debacle might have been prevented. It highlights the need for strict oversight of how partners and contractors use data: contracts and APIs should have not only rules but active enforcement and audits. It also emphasizes the necessity of clear consent mechanisms – users should know and agree to what happens with their data. In the aftermath, Facebook tightened its platform policies and limited data access for apps, but only after the horse had bolted from the barn.

Another lesson is that ethical foresight is crucial. Facebook's team likely did not *intend* for user data to be misused for electioneering, but they failed to imagine how their platform could be exploited. Conducting ethics reviews or "red team" exercises to brainstorm possible abuses might have raised red flags (for example: what if someone uses our data for political manipulation or discrimination?). Ethical scenario planning can help companies anticipate and guard against worst-case outcomes of data practices.

Finally, this case shows that regulatory and legal consequences for ethical lapses in AI/data can be enormous. A $5B fine and new regulatory scrutiny (not to mention impending laws like GDPR, which came into effect shortly after) demonstrate that government bodies are willing to act when companies violate public trust. Organizations should view ethical data practices as part of compliance and risk management. The cost of building privacy and ethics into products is far less than the cost of a scandal.

- *Key Takeaways (Facebook & Cambridge Analytica):*

  o **Treat data as a privilege, not a right:** User data should be handled with care, and shared only with strict oversight. Facebook's loose data-sharing allowed a third party to abuse information from millions of users without their knowledge. Managers must ensure robust data governance – know where data goes and why.

  o **Informed consent is non-negotiable:** Every user should know what they are consenting to. In this case, users did *not* consent to political use of their data. Ethical businesses provide transparency and choice to users about data usage, avoiding any sneaky or indirect data collection.

o **Anticipate misuse:** Companies need to proactively imagine how their platforms or data could be misused. The Cambridge Analytica saga reveals that bad actors can repurpose data in harmful ways. Regular ethical risk assessments could have identified the danger of data being used to manipulate public opinion, prompting preventative action.

o **Swift action and accountability:** When a breach or misuse is discovered, respond quickly and openly. Facebook's delayed response and initial denials exacerbated public anger. An ethical organization acknowledges problems, fixes them, and communicates honestly.

o **Regulatory compliance and beyond:** Laws and regulations (like privacy laws) set the minimum standard. Going beyond compliance – embracing digital ethics as a core value – can save a company from disaster. If Facebook had heeded its 2012 FTC agreement more earnestly, it might have avoided the $5B fine and loss of user trust. The scandal ultimately reinforced that ethical lapses have real financial and legal repercussions, and protecting user data is both a moral duty and a business imperative.

Facing the Facials: IBM's Stand on Facial Recognition

Not all case studies in tech ethics are about failures or scandals. In some instances, companies proactively make ethical choices that set positive examples. One such instance is IBM's decision in 2020 to step back from the facial recognition business. Facial recognition technology (FRT) had become increasingly controversial due to concerns about privacy violations, mass surveillance, and racial bias. The tipping point came amid global protests over racial injustice (following the killing of George Floyd in May 2020) when technology companies were under pressure to ensure their tools were not contributing to oppression. In June 2020, IBM's CEO Arvind Krishna made a landmark announcement: IBM would no longer offer general-purpose facial recognition or analysis software and would halt all research & development in this area.

IBM explicitly cited ethical reasons for this decision. In a letter to the U.S. Congress, Krishna wrote that IBM "firmly opposes and will not condone" the use of facial recognition technology for purposes that violate human rights and freedoms. This included mass surveillance, racial profiling, and other uses that were inconsistent with the company's values and principles of trust and transparency. Essentially, IBM was saying: *Just because we can build this technology doesn't mean we will – not if it can be used to oppress people.* IBM also urged Congress to begin a national dialogue on how facial recognition should be regulated, signaling that current laws and regulations were insufficient to ensure responsible use.

Why was facial recognition singled out? By 2020, multiple studies had shown that many facial recognition systems, including some of the best-known ones, had significant accuracy disparities across different demographic groups. Research by MIT's Joy Buolamwini and others famously found that algorithms had much higher error rates in identifying dark-skinned faces, especially dark-skinned women, compared to white male faces. This raised the risk of false arrests or misidentifications of minorities. Moreover, around the world, law enforcement agencies were starting to deploy facial recognition without clear regulations, raising fears of an AI-driven surveillance state. Civil liberties groups warned that without oversight, facial recognition could enable "Orwellian" mass surveillance and exacerbate racial bias in policing. IBM, with its long history in the technology sector, presumably weighed these factors and decided that the potential for misuse outweighed the potential revenue from selling such systems. In the words of IBM's CEO, the technology could be used in ways "not consistent with our values," and so they drew an ethical line in the sand.

IBM's stand was significant for several reasons. First, it was a rare instance of a big tech company voluntarily foregoing a technology because of ethics. This wasn't prompted by a scandal or legal requirement — it was preemptive ethical leadership. IBM was one of the pioneers of facial recognition technology, yet it chose principles over profit in this domain. Second, IBM's move put pressure on its industry peers. In the immediate aftermath, other tech giants responded: Amazon announced a one-year moratorium on police use of its "Rekognition" facial recognition software, and Microsoft likewise said it would pause sales of its facial recognition tech to police until federal regulations were in place. In essence, IBM's decision sparked an industry-wide reflection on the responsible use of facial recognition. It gave cover for others to follow suit, and it fueled public debate. Lawmakers referenced these corporate stances when pushing for clearer rules. Indeed, IBM actively called for legislation – rather than just quietly exiting, the company used its voice to advocate for societal guidelines.

The reaction to IBM's announcement was largely positive. Advocacy groups and civil rights organizations praised IBM for putting ethics first, highlighting that this was the strongest statement to date by a major tech firm against the misuse of AI surveillance. IBM's decision was seen as aligning the company with the values of racial justice and privacy at a critical moment. It also helped rehabilitate IBM's image as a trustworthy, socially responsible innovator, which is valuable for long-term brand reputation. Some skeptics pointed out that IBM's facial recognition market share was smaller compared to competitors (IBM wasn't the top provider of these systems in 2020). They questioned whether the decision was purely ethical or partly strategic. However, even if market position made it easier, IBM set a precedent: it demonstrated that tech companies *can* choose to withdraw a technology on ethical grounds, not just when forced by regulation.

For managers, IBM's stance on facial recognition is inspiring and instructive. It shows that ethical leadership often means taking initiative – not waiting for laws or crises, but acting because it's the right thing to do and aligns with your organization's values. This might involve some short-term sacrifice. In IBM's case, they gave up current and future business in a technology that could be lucrative (many governments and agencies are interested in facial recognition tools). However, the decision can yield long-term gains in trust and goodwill, which are harder to quantify but immensely important. It also illustrates the concept of an "ethical line in the sand." IBM determined that certain uses of AI (like unwarranted surveillance) crossed a line they were not willing to be on the wrong side of. Each company may have to determine its own lines based on its values and the expectations of its stakeholders.

Finally, IBM's move underscores the role of corporate influence in policy. By publicly exiting and urging regulation, IBM added momentum to the call for responsible AI policies. Managers should recognize that they can play a role in shaping the ethical landscape of their industry — sometimes self-regulation and bold public commitments can drive change faster than waiting for external rules.

- *Key Takeaways (IBM & Facial Recognition):*
  - **Principles before profit:** IBM's withdrawal from facial recognition demonstrates that foregoing a business opportunity may be warranted if the ethical risks are too high. This act of principle won IBM commendations for prioritizing human rights and privacy over short-term revenue. It's a powerful example to other businesses that ethics can guide strategic decisions.
  - **Industry leadership and influence:** One company's ethical stance can influence an entire industry. IBM's

decision prompted competitors to re-evaluate their own policies (e.g. Amazon and Microsoft pausing law enforcement sales). Managers should not underestimate how taking a stand can set a new norm and encourage broader responsible behavior.

○ **Acknowledging societal impact:** IBM recognized the potential for harm in its technology (racial profiling, mass surveillance) and took accountability for it. Ethical management means anticipating how your products could be misused and acting to prevent that — even if misuse is by third parties (e.g., governments) rather than the company itself.

○ **Call for regulation:** Rather than resisting regulation, IBM actively called for laws to guide AI use. In fast-moving fields like AI, gaps in regulation exist; responsible companies can fill the void by creating their own strict guidelines and advocating for public policy, showing that they welcome rules that ensure fairness and protect rights.

○ **Trust as an asset:** By taking an ethical stand, IBM likely bolstered trust among customers, partners, and the public. In an era of rising concern over AI, being seen as a company that self-polices for ethics can be a competitive advantage. Managers should view ethical reputation as an asset — hard to build, easy to lose.

Investing in it through principled actions is as important as any R&D investment.

Each of these case studies — Amazon, Apple Card, Facebook/Cambridge Analytica, and IBM — makes the need for human-centered AI vividly clear. They show that ethical considerations in algorithms are not theoretical niceties but practical requirements for success and sustainability in business. Whether it's ensuring fairness in hiring, equity in financial services, privacy in data use, or integrity in how technology is deployed, the lesson is the same: Ethics in action is a fundamental part of making principled decisions in a data-driven world. By learning from these real-world examples, managers can better anticipate challenges and champion ethical AI practices within their own organizations, leading the way in an era where doing what is right is integral to doing good business.

Chapter 7
Implementing Digital Ethics in Your Organization

Implementing digital ethics is about translating principles into everyday business practices. This chapter provides practical guidance for managers to embed ethical AI into their organization's structures and culture. By establishing governance teams, fostering an ethical culture, integrating "ethics by design" in development, and maintaining ongoing accountability, even a small company can make principled decisions in a data-driven world. The tone here is encouraging and pragmatic: perfect ethical AI may be unattainable, but every organization can take appropriate steps to do the right thing with AI.

Building an AI Ethics Governance Team

A strong governance framework is the foundation of ethical AI implementation. Many executives recognize its importance – for example, a Gartner study found 79% of executives say AI ethics is important, yet less than 25% have operationalized ethical governance. To close this gap, organizations should create a dedicated AI ethics governance team or committee to oversee high-impact AI projects. This team's role is to ensure that AI initiatives are reviewed for ethical risks and aligned with company values and policies. Even if your organization is not a tech giant, you can establish governance measures scaled to your size and industry. Below are key steps and considerations for building an AI ethics governance program:

1. **Secure Leadership Commitment:** Start by getting buy-in from top leadership. Ethical AI requires tone from the top, so identify an executive sponsor who believes in responsible innovation. This could be a Chief Technology Officer, Chief Data Officer, Chief Ethics Officer, or any C-level champion passionate about digital ethics. Leadership support ensures the initiative has authority and resources, and signals to the whole company that ethical AI is a priority.

2. **Define Roles and Responsibilities:** Clearly assign who will be responsible for AI ethics oversight. Many organizations form an AI ethics committee or board that includes leaders from various departments (e.g. IT, data science, legal, compliance, HR). The committee's mandate is to review and approve high-impact AI systems, policies, and incidents. In addition, designate specific roles – for instance, a *Responsible AI Lead* or *ethics officer* – to coordinate efforts. In large enterprises, each business unit might appoint an *AI ethics champion* to act as a liaison. The goal is to have named people accountable for monitoring ethical risks in AI projects.

3. **Include Diverse, Cross-Functional Members:** Ethical AI governance works best when it brings together diverse perspectives. Make sure the governance team isn't just engineers or data scientists. Include representatives from legal (to address

compliance), privacy/security (for data protection concerns), HR (for workforce implications), and potentially marketing or customer experience (to consider user impacts). If possible, invite an independent voice such as an external ethicist or a member of an underrepresented group to provide outsider perspective. A mix of backgrounds will help the team foresee issues that a single-discipline group might miss, and ensure decisions consider social and human impacts from multiple angles.

4. **Establish Processes for Ethical Review:** Define how the governance team will operate. For example, institute a requirement that any AI project above a certain risk level (e.g. affecting customers or involving sensitive data) must go through an ethics review checkpoint. The team could hold regular meetings to review proposals, conduct risk assessments, and approve or recommend changes to projects. Create documentation templates for these reviews – e.g. an "AI Ethics Impact Assessment" form that project teams must fill out detailing the system's purpose, data used, potential biases, and mitigation plans. By having a standardized review workflow, ethics checks become a routine part of project governance rather than an afterthought.

5. **Provide Escalation Paths:** Ensure there is a clear path to escalate concerns. If an employee or team identifies an ethical risk they cannot resolve, they should know how to bring it to the AI ethics committee's attention. This might involve a hotline or a

formal issue submission process. The governance team in turn should have support from top executives or a board committee, so that serious issues (like an AI system possibly causing legal or reputational harm) can be addressed swiftly at the highest levels. In essence, build an escalation ladder from frontline staff up to the executive level, to handle ethical dilemmas in AI development or deployment.

A real-world example of robust AI ethics governance comes from IBM's approach. IBM has built a multilayered AI ethics governance framework with distinct roles at each level. At the top, a Policy Advisory Committee of senior leaders sets strategy and provides oversight of AI ethics initiatives. Next, an AI Ethics Board – a cross-disciplinary central body – manages a centralized review and decision-making process for AI ethics issues across IBM's products, services, and research. To ensure ethical practice permeates all business units, IBM appointed AI Ethics Focal Points in each unit: these are trained representatives who act as the first line of contact to identify ethical concerns in AI use cases and mitigate risks, escalating issues to the central board if needed. Finally, IBM created an Advocacy Network of employees across different workstreams who champion and spread IBM's ethics principles at the grassroots level. This network helps scale ethical awareness and "eyes on the ground" throughout the company. Together, these elements – an executive committee, a core ethics board, unit-level focal points, and an employee network – illustrate a comprehensive governance stack ensuring AI projects are vetted for alignment with IBM's values and the evolving regulatory landscape.

Such an extensive structure might sound out of reach for a smaller organization, but the underlying idea is adaptable. Even a small or mid-sized company can start with a modest governance setup. For example, you might have a single Responsible AI Officer or committee that meets quarterly to review projects. If a dedicated committee is too much, integrate ethical review into an existing governance body – for instance, add AI ethics to the agenda of your IT governance committee or risk management team. The key is to formalize responsibility: identify who (an individual or group) will be accountable for checking that AI applications are fair, transparent, and compliant. Small firms can also leverage external resources: consult industry guidelines or even form a shared ethics panel with a partner or advisor. The tone to strike with your team is that *any organization can start governance measures appropriate to its size*. Whether it's one person wearing the ethics hat or a board with sub-committees, doing *something* is far better than nothing. By setting up basic governance, you establish ownership of AI ethics and send a message to all employees that ethical considerations are an integral part of doing business with AI.

Fostering an Ethical AI Culture

Governance structures alone will not ensure ethical AI – the organization's culture and people are just as important as any policy or tool. Fostering an ethical AI culture means making ethics "part of the DNA" of the company, rather than a box-ticking exercise. Everyone from engineers to executives to end-users should be aware of ethical risks and feel empowered to act responsibly. This section provides guidance on education, awareness, and everyday practices that build a culture of ethical AI. The message is that *every employee has a role in AI ethics*, and by training and engagement, ethics becomes a shared value rather than an afterthought.

1. Education and Training for All: Begin by educating your workforce about AI ethics principles and issues. This goes beyond the data science team – *every* employee interacting with AI outputs or customer data should have a basic understanding of risks like bias, privacy, and security. Consider running regular workshops or training sessions on topics such as identifying AI bias, protecting user privacy, and cybersecurity in AI systems. These could be scenario-based sessions where teams discuss hypothetical ethical dilemmas, or lunchtime talks about recent AI ethics incidents in the news. Training should be accessible and relevant: for instance, your sales and HR teams might get examples on how AI could unintentionally discriminate in pricing or hiring, whereas engineers get deeper sessions on fairness metrics and model transparency. The goal is to raise awareness company-wide so that ethical red flags are recognized early by anyone, not just specialists. Proper training and awareness can meaningfully reduce risks – it helps employees use AI tools responsibly and avoid pitfalls. As one industry guide notes, educating staff on AI's limitations and risks *mitigates bias and compliance issues* while empowering them to leverage AI safely. Making ethics a frequent topic of discussion signals that it's a core expectation, not an optional add-on.

2. Encourage Open Dialogue and Reporting: An ethical culture thrives when employees feel comfortable voicing concerns. Create channels for open dialogue about AI projects and their societal impact. This could mean setting up an "AI Ethics Office Hours" where anyone can ask questions or suggest improvements to an AI system. Encourage employees to flag ethical issues (like noticing a biased output or a use of personal data that feels invasive) without fear of retaliation. In fact, *celebrate and reward employees who speak up* – for example, acknowledge in company communications when a team member identified a bias in a model and helped fix it. This positive reinforcement shows that identifying ethical risks is seen as a valuable contribution to the company's success, not as hindering progress. Some organizations incorporate this into performance evaluations, by including ethical considerations in project post-mortems or KPIs. For instance, a product team might be evaluated not just on delivery and revenue, but also on metrics like user trust or lack of ethical incidents. By integrating ethical behavior into performance goals, you send a clear message: how results are achieved (fairly and responsibly) is as important as achieving the results. Additionally, leadership should lead by example in transparency – when ethical concerns are raised, leaders ought to communicate what is being done to address them. This openness builds trust and reinforces that ethics isn't about blame, it's about continuous improvement.

3. Build Diverse Teams and Inclusive Design Processes: One of the strongest safeguards against one-sided AI outcomes is to involve diverse people in building and testing AI. Teams that include people of different genders, ethnic backgrounds, ages, disciplines, and life experiences are far less likely to produce products that overlook or disadvantage certain groups. Conversely, homogenous teams can inadvertently bake in their blind spots. Research strongly supports this: diversity in the AI community makes it easier to spot biases and blind spots – often, the first people to notice a bias are those from the affected minority group. Therefore, make diversity a priority in hiring and team formation for AI projects. If your development group isn't diverse, seek input from other staff or external advisors who can represent different perspectives. You might also implement practices like inclusive design reviews, where a diverse panel reviews AI prototypes specifically to catch unfair or insensitive outcomes. In short, *varied eyes on the problem lead to more balanced AI solutions.* Beyond team composition, cultivate an inclusive mindset: remind your creators to think about how an AI feature might impact someone *unlike* themselves. This can be as simple as asking during design meetings, "Who might be harmed or excluded by this technology, and have we considered their needs?" By fostering empathy and inclusion in the creation process, you reduce the chances of one-sided biases echoing in the final product.

4. Integrate Ethics into Daily Work and Values: Truly embedding ethics in the culture means it should show up in everyday work and in the company's core values. Organizations can take concrete steps to weave ethics into the fabric of operations. For example, include ethical guidelines in your standard operating procedures for AI projects – make it a habit that every project kickoff starts with discussing potential ethical issues (we'll discuss this more in "Ethics by Design"). Some companies update their Code of Conduct or corporate values to explicitly mention responsible use of AI and data. A notable example is Scotiabank: the bank established a data ethics policy and then made it part of the company's Code of Conduct, which every employee must attest to annually. This kind of measure formally cements ethical AI as a non-negotiable principle of doing business. You can also incorporate ethics into onboarding for new employees and into leadership development programs. Recognize and highlight positive examples – e.g. feature a "story of the month" where an AI product team took an extra step to ensure fairness or where an employee's caution prevented a potential privacy issue. Over time, these practices create a virtuous cycle: employees see that acting ethically is valued and expected, which encourages more ethical action, and so on. The cultural norm becomes that ethics is everyone's job, not just the compliance officer's. When ethics is ingrained in daily decisions and celebrated in the company, you have achieved a culture where doing the right thing with AI is second nature.

In summary, building an ethical AI culture is about people and values. Provide the knowledge and tools (training, discussion forums, resources) so employees can act ethically. Promote diversity and inclusion so that your AI reflects broad perspectives. And make ethical considerations a routine part of work life – from goal-setting to recognition. An organization with a strong ethics culture will be far more resilient in the face of AI's challenges, because its people will instinctively uphold principles even when no one is watching. This human factor is as critical as any technical fix in achieving trustworthy AI.

Ethics by Design in AI Development

To truly implement digital ethics, organizations must bake ethics into every stage of AI development – from the initial idea to deployment and beyond. This section lays out a blueprint for "ethics by design," meaning that ethical risk checks are integrated into the standard workflow of developing AI systems. By following a structured process (which can be facilitated with checklists or templates, some of which we provide later in this book), managers can ensure that ethical considerations are addressed systematically rather than in an ad hoc way. The approach is similar to how one might incorporate security or quality assurance: proactive, continuous, and documented. Below, we outline key phases of the AI development lifecycle and how to embed ethics in each:

1. Project Inception – Ethical Risk Assessment: Ethical AI design begins at the project kickoff. When scoping a new AI product or feature, include an *ethical risk assessment* alongside business and technical assessments. This means asking foundational questions: *What is the purpose of this AI system? Who could be affected by it, and how? What could go wrong or be misused?* At this stage, some organizations use a formal Algorithmic Impact Assessment (AIA) or "bias impact statement," analogous to a privacy impact assessment or environmental impact report. For example, the Brookings Institution recommends that teams develop a bias impact statement at project start to probe potential biases and harms. Such a statement or checklist prompts the team to consider the algorithm's intended outcome, the data it will use, and who might be disproportionately impacted. It often includes questions like: "Which decisions will this AI make? Who is the audience or user, and who is most affected by the outcomes? Could there be disparate impact or unfair treatment for certain groups? How will we test for and mitigate bias? What is our plan if something goes wrong?". Engaging in this kind of structured brainstorming early can avert harmful impacts before any code is written. Importantly, this kickoff should involve a cross-functional team – not just developers but also stakeholders like legal or ethics advisors, domain experts, and representatives of affected users. Their diverse insights during planning will highlight ethical risks that might otherwise be missed. By the end of inception, the project should have a clear understanding of its ethical risk profile and a plan (or at least guiding principles) for how those risks will be managed.

2. Data Collection & Preparation – Guardrails for Privacy and Fairness: The next stage in an AI project typically involves gathering data or defining data sources. Here, apply "data ethics by design" principles. Ensure any data collection respects privacy and user consent. Ask: *Are we gathering this data with proper notice and consent from users? Is all this data necessary for our purpose (data minimization)? Are we complying with regulations like GDPR in handling personal data?* Good practice is to limit data to what you truly need and anonymize or protect sensitive information as early as possible. For example, under GDPR and similar laws, organizations are mandated to implement data protection by design, which includes practices like data minimization, ensuring data accuracy, and confidentiality from the outset. In concrete terms, this might mean building consent checkpoints into apps that collect data, providing opt-outs for users, and running privacy impact assessments on datasets.

Additionally, *think about bias in the data.* If you're curating a training dataset, put guardrails to ensure it's representative and fair. For instance, if an AI will be used in hiring, make sure the training data isn't just past employees (which could encode past discrimination). You might set guidelines like: include data from a mix of demographics, or balance the dataset so that minority classes are sufficiently represented. Tools can help here – some teams use data sheets or datasheets for datasets that document the composition of data and any identified biases. By treating data ethics as a first-class concern (just like data quality), you prevent a host of downstream problems. Key guardrail questions at this stage: *Do we have the right to use this data? Are we respecting individuals' rights? Is the data skewed or incomplete in ways that could lead to unfair outcomes?* Catching these issues now is much easier than fixing a trained model later.

3. Model Development – Bias Testing and Fairness Checks: As the project moves into model building and experimentation, embed testing for ethical criteria alongside performance metrics. Data scientists and developers should not only ask "How accurate is this model?" but also "Is it fair and transparent?" One recommended practice is to perform bias testing on models – in other words, evaluate the model's outputs across different groups to see if there are disparities. For example, if building a credit scoring model, test its predictions for male vs. female applicants, or for different ethnic groups (using proxy variables if needed), to check whether error rates or approval rates differ significantly. If the model is "blind" to those attributes, it may still inadvertently treat groups differently via proxies. In fact, experts note that *actively measuring protected attributes* (like gender or race) during testing is necessary to ensure an algorithm isn't discriminatory. One high-profile analysis by the Brookings Institution advised companies to examine both the data fed to algorithms *and* the algorithm's outcomes to detect bias – for instance, check if an AI's decisions systematically favor one group over another, or if error rates are higher for a minority group. So during model validation, incorporate fairness metrics such as disparate impact (ratio of outcomes between groups) or use tools like confusion matrices broken down by subgroup. There are also emerging toolkits (IBM's AI Fairness 360, Google's What-If Tool, etc.) that can help scan for bias in models. If biases are found, iterate on the model – this might involve collecting more diverse training data, adjusting the model's parameters or algorithm (e.g. adding fairness constraints), or even deciding not to use a model if it's inherently too problematic. Beyond bias, consider explainability at this stage: use interpretable models or add explanation techniques so you (and users/regulators) can understand why the AI makes the decisions it does. Document the choices you make: for instance, keep a record if you decided to exclude a certain attribute to avoid bias, or if you calibrated the model to correct an imbalance. By the end of development, you should have not just a high-performing model, but one that has been vetted for ethical quality – with evidence (test results, documentation) to back it up.

4. Pre-Deployment – Review, Validation, and Approval: Before an AI system goes live, have a final ethical review checkpoint. This can be handled by the AI ethics governance team or a specific review board. Treat it like a "go/no-go" gate focused on ethics and compliance. The reviewers should verify that all the steps above were followed: Was an ethical risk assessment done and all high risks addressed? Does the latest bias testing show acceptable results (e.g. no severe biases remain)? Do we have mitigation plans for potential failures (if the AI makes a wrong decision, how will we detect and correct it)? Also, ensure compliance checks: for instance, if the AI will be deployed in the EU, does it meet the requirements of regulations like GDPR or the upcoming EU AI Act? If it's a high-risk application (like in healthcare or finance), should you conduct an external audit or seek certification before deployment? Some organizations institute an *"Algorithmic Ethics Checklist"* that must be completed and signed off by the project lead and the ethics officer. This might include items like: *Data collection was lawful and consensual; Model was tested for bias on X, Y, Z demographics; Results were peer-reviewed by an internal committee; Model interpretability documentation (e.g. model card) is completed; Monitoring plan for post-deployment is in place.* By systematically reviewing such a list, you ensure nothing slips through the cracks at launch. A best practice example comes from Scotiabank's approach: they created an Ethics Assessment tool (in partnership with an external firm) that evaluates an AI use case's ethical implications before it is fully deployed. Running this "ethics check" is mandatory as the first step for all new AI projects at the bank, and if it flags issues, the project must adjust its design before proceeding. This kind of process institutionalizes ethics by design. In your organization, you might not have a fancy tool, but a well-crafted checklist or a small review committee can fulfill a similar function. The outcome of the pre-deployment review could be approval, conditional approval (with some changes required), or a denial/postponement if major ethical risks are unresolved. It's better to delay or tweak a product than to launch something that could cause harm or backlash.

5. Deployment and Ongoing Monitoring: Ethics by design doesn't stop at launch – it continues into deployment and operations (which overlaps with the next section on continuous oversight). Ensure that the system is launched with proper guardrails and monitoring active. For example, implement real-time alerts if the model starts drifting or making out-of-bounds predictions, so you can intervene. Set up a feedback loop: allow users or internal auditors to report if the AI output seems wrong or unfair. Some companies perform a post-deployment audit a few months in, to validate that the model in production behaves as expected on real-world data. The Brookings report we mentioned earlier advocates for ongoing audits and even feedback mechanisms that involve external stakeholders or civil society in evaluating algorithms' impacts. In practice, this might mean periodically re-checking bias metrics with new data, or inviting an external ethics consultant to review the system after it's been in use. The core idea is to not adopt a "fire-and-forget" mentality with AI systems – responsible managers assume that ethical risks evolve and require continuous vigilance. By planning for monitoring and maintenance at the design stage, you avoid the trap of thinking the ethics job is "done" at deployment. Instead, ethics is a lifecycle commitment.

By following this blueprint – starting with ethical planning, enforcing ethical data practices, rigorously testing models for fairness, and reviewing thoroughly before deployment – organizations can operationalize ethics at every step. It turns what could be abstract principles ("avoid bias", "respect privacy") into concrete tasks and checkpoints in your project plan. Having these processes in place also prepares you for regulatory compliance: for example, if new laws require algorithmic transparency or impact assessments, you'll already be doing it. Remember that tools like checklists, templates, and frameworks are there to help – feel free to adapt the ones provided in this book or from external frameworks (such as the Brookings bias impact statement template or industry guidelines) to fit your workflows. Over time, as your team gets used to this way of working, "ethics by design" will simply become second nature in your product development, much like "security by design" or quality assurance. This structured approach ensures that ethical considerations are not left to chance or addressed in a panic at the end – they are built into the product, just like any other key feature.

Accountability and Continuous Oversight

Implementing digital ethics is not a one-and-done effort – it requires ongoing accountability and oversight to sustain ethical performance over time. AI systems can change (models drift, data evolves) and business contexts shift (new regulations, new use cases), so an organization must continuously monitor and adjust its AI for ethical alignment. In this final section of the chapter, we discuss how to maintain accountability through clear ownership, regular audits, metrics tracking, and staying ahead of external requirements. The tone is pragmatic: no system will ever be perfect, and issues will arise, but with the right oversight processes, you can catch problems early and respond effectively. By building feedback loops and accountability structures, you ensure that ethical AI is not just a project, but an enduring practice.

1. Assign Clear "Owners" for AI Systems: A crucial aspect of accountability is knowing who is responsible for what. Every significant AI system or product in your organization should have a designated *owner* (or a team) accountable for its ethical behavior and compliance. This is akin to having a product owner or system manager, but with a specific mandate for ethical oversight. The owner's duties would include monitoring the system's outputs for problems, coordinating bias or performance audits, handling any incident responses, and ensuring the system adheres to policies and laws. Establishing such roles resonates with best-practice frameworks – for instance, the U.S. NIST AI Risk Management Framework emphasizes accountability as a pillar, defined by clear roles, responsibilities, and governance structures to manage AI risks. In practice, this could mean your Head of Data Science is the accountable owner for all machine learning models in production, or you might assign ownership at a system level (e.g. the HR analytics manager owns the recruiting AI tool's ethics). For smaller projects, the project manager or product manager can carry this responsibility. What's important is that everyone knows who the point person is for a given AI system's ethical compliance. This prevents issues from falling through the cracks. If, say, an AI-driven loan approval system starts getting complaints of bias, there is a clear individual who must investigate and address it. Owners should also maintain documentation (like an ethics log or model history) for their systems, which aids transparency and accountability. In sum, *make accountability explicit*: map out your AI inventory and assign names to each – it creates a culture where people take ownership and pride in maintaining the integrity of "their" AI system.

2. Conduct Regular Audits and Evaluations: Just as financial accounts are audited periodically, AI systems benefit from regular ethical audits. These can be annual or more frequent depending on the risk profile of the system. An AI audit involves re-evaluating the system's performance on criteria like fairness, accuracy, privacy, and transparency. Over time, data distributions can shift or new usage patterns emerge that introduce biases not seen at launch. A structured audit will catch these changes. For example, you might discover that a model's accuracy for a certain group has degraded as new data came in, prompting a retraining. Audits should also review compliance with any updated regulations or standards. It's wise to use checklists or frameworks for audits – you might revisit the same questions from the design phase (impact assessments, etc.) and see if anything has changed. Involving an independent reviewer can add credibility; some firms engage external auditors or academics to evaluate their algorithms impartially. Brookings experts have suggested that thorough audits, potentially including third-party input and feedback from those impacted by the algorithm, are key to detecting and deterring biases. This reflects a growing trend: "algorithmic auditing" is becoming a recognized practice, and regulators are increasingly interested in it. Internally, you can create an audit team (perhaps a subset of the ethics committee or internal audit department) to carry this out. After each audit, document the findings and track the implementation of any recommended fixes. These audits not only help maintain fairness and accuracy, but also serve as evidence to regulators, investors, or customers that the company is serious about responsible AI.

3. Track Ethics Metrics and Performance Indicators: In addition to qualitative reviews, define some quantitative metrics to gauge your AI's ethical performance over time. Earlier, we embedded ethics into design and culture; now we measure it. What could these metrics be? One category is *bias and fairness metrics* – for instance, measure the disparity in outcomes between demographic groups for key decisions (approval rates, error rates, etc.). If you have a threshold (say, the model's false-positive rate for any group should not exceed 1.5 times that of another), track that over time. Another approach is to use formal metrics proposed in research: some organizations compute a "bias detection score" or "fairness score" for their models, which quantify how balanced the model's performance is across groups. These scores can be part of regular reports. Accountability can also be tracked via process metrics: for example, how many AI projects completed an ethics review checklist, how many bias issues were identified and corrected before launch, how many were found after launch, and how quickly they were fixed. You might also gauge employee engagement in ethics (number of concerns raised, training completion rates) as a proxy for culture health. A particularly interesting high-level metric is the Model Accountability Index (MAI) introduced in some frameworks, which measures how well an AI system complies with legal standards and policies. Essentially, it's an index of the system's adherence to various accountability criteria. While such an index might be complex to calculate, even a simplified scorecard can help you benchmark progress. The exact metrics will vary by industry – a healthcare AI might track patient safety incidents or diagnostic equity, whereas a social media AI might track the percentage of content flagged and actioned for policy violations. The point is to treat ethics like any other performance dimension: define targets or acceptable ranges, and monitor them just as you would uptime or revenue. This also enables continuous improvement – if an ethics metric shows a dip (say, a rising bias trend), it flags the need for intervention.

4. Align with Evolving Regulations and Standards: The external environment for AI ethics is dynamic. Laws, regulations, and industry standards around AI are rapidly emerging – from privacy laws to algorithmic transparency requirements to sector-specific guidelines. It's crucial that your oversight practices keep your organization ahead of compliance needs. Assign a team or individual (perhaps within the legal or compliance department, or the AI governance group) to monitor regulatory developments. This involves tracking new legislation like the European Union's AI Act, updates to data protection laws, or guidance from bodies like the OECD or ISO on AI governance. Effective AI governance requires adhering to these evolving rules and even anticipating them. For instance, international frameworks such as the OECD AI Principles stress concepts like inclusive growth, human-centered values, fairness, and transparency – your accountability practices can be mapped to these principles to ensure you're aligned with global best practices. If a new law is on the horizon (say a law mandating the right to explanation for algorithmic decisions), you might start incorporating that into your systems now (e.g. building explanation features) rather than scrambling later. Regularly update your internal policies to reflect the latest legal requirements – perhaps your data ethics policy gets an annual refresh. Moreover, engage with industry consortiums or ethics advocacy groups to stay informed and contribute. The idea is to future-proof your ethical AI program: continuous oversight includes scanning the horizon for what "ethical" will mean tomorrow. Companies that do this can turn compliance into a competitive advantage – they will not only avoid penalties but also earn trust by being early adopters of high standards. Remember, AI accountability is increasingly *not optional*: regulators worldwide are sending the message that organizations must be able to demonstrate how they manage AI risks. By proactively aligning with these expectations, you ensure your organization is prepared and can confidently show stakeholders that your AI is under control.

5. Expect Imperfection and Plan for Incident Response: Despite best efforts, no AI system is flawless and ethical challenges will arise. Accountability means acknowledging this and having a plan for when things go wrong. Part of continuous oversight is setting up an AI incident response process. Similar to IT incident response, define steps to take if an AI system causes an unexpected harm or major error. For example, if an AI makes a discriminatory decision that creates a PR crisis, who convenes to address it? How will you communicate with affected parties? Having a playbook ready will save precious time and demonstrate accountability. Also consider a mechanism for "turning off" or rolling back an AI system if it's deemed unsafe – owners should know the kill-switch procedures. Document incidents and lessons learned, and feed that back into improving your design and governance processes (closing the loop). An accountable organization is one that, when faced with an ethical failure, transparently investigates the cause, fixes it, and updates its practices so it doesn't happen again. Importantly, don't punish teams or hide issues when they occur – treat them as learning opportunities to strengthen the system. Over time, a cycle of monitor -> detect -> respond -> improve will create a robust ethical assurance process. And by openly addressing issues, you build credibility with regulators and the public. Remember the pragmatic view: perfection is impossible in complex AI systems, but what stakeholders and regulators want to see is that you are *managing* the imperfections responsibly. Continuous oversight means just that – continuously watching, evaluating, and adapting your AI in pursuit of ethical quality.

In conclusion, implementing digital ethics in an organization is an ongoing journey. By establishing clear accountability for AI systems, regularly auditing and measuring their ethical performance, and staying aligned with societal standards, managers can maintain control over AI's impact. The tools and practices discussed – governance teams, culture programs, ethics-by-design workflows, and oversight mechanisms – collectively form a toolkit that any organization can tailor to its needs. An ethical AI program is not about never making a mistake; it's about having the principles, processes, and people in place to do the right thing when it counts. In the next chapters, we will continue to provide resources (including templates for documentation and audit checklists) to help operationalize these ideas. By taking the practical steps outlined in this chapter, you as a manager can lead your organization toward human-centered AI that not only achieves business goals but also upholds the values we care about in a data-driven world.

Chapter 8

The Road Ahead – Making Principled Decisions in a Data-Driven World

Emerging Challenges and Opportunities

As artificial intelligence continues to advance, managers face a wave of new challenges – but also promising opportunities – in the data-driven world. One prominent trend is the rise of generative AI systems, such as advanced chatbots and content generators. These tools can produce text, images, and even synthetic media with astonishing realism. Yet their ethical quirks are becoming clear. For example, today's large language models have a well-documented tendency to "hallucinate" – in other words, they occasionally fabricate false or misleading information in very confident ways. In fact, evaluations like the TruthfulQA benchmark show many generative models are truthful only about 25% of the time. This means that, roughly speaking, an AI like a chatbot may give incorrect or made-up answers far more often than not, which poses serious risks if managers rely on such outputs unchecked. A conversational agent might present a fictitious "fact" or a non-existent legal case as if it were true, potentially misleading decision-makers or customers. Addressing this truthfulness challenge is critical – organizations will need rigorous verification processes and human oversight to ensure AI-generated content is accurate before it influences business decisions. The flip side is that improving AI's truthfulness presents an opportunity: companies investing in more transparent and reliable AI (for instance, systems that can explain their sources or admit uncertainty) could differentiate themselves by providing tools that augment human decision-making without the misinformation.

Beyond content generation, AI is expanding into new domains of business, each raising novel ethical questions. Consider algorithmic hiring – using AI to screen résumés or even conduct video interviews. Done right, this promises efficiency and objectivity; however, real-world cases show it can easily go wrong. In one instance, a large online retailer built a hiring algorithm to identify top engineering candidates, only to discover that the system had learned to systematically disfavor female applicants. Trained on ten years of past résumés from a male-dominated tech industry, the AI model "taught itself" that male candidates were preferable and even penalized resumes containing the word "women's," such as "women's chess club captain". This biased outcome was not due to any ill intent by developers, but rather an unchecked training process that mirrored historical inequities. The company ultimately scrapped the tool, recognizing that an uncorrected AI could unfairly perpetuate discrimination. The lesson for managers is that AI in hiring must be approached with extreme care – data and algorithms should be audited for bias, and transparency is key so that candidates and recruiters understand how decisions are made. Yet, there is an opportunity here as well: when designed with fairness in mind, AI hiring tools could actually help reduce human biases. For example, some firms now use AI to remove identifying information from job applications or to flag biased language in job postings, helping recruiters focus on qualifications rather than demographic factors. By standardizing the evaluation criteria and scrutinizing language for hidden biases, AI can assist in widening the talent pool and promoting diversity. In short, if managers cultivate inclusive training data and put guardrails in place, algorithmic hiring could become a means to mitigate the very biases that traditional hiring often struggles with.

Another frontier is the use of AI in surveillance and security. Advances in facial recognition and predictive analytics have made it possible to monitor public spaces or analyze video feeds at an unprecedented scale. The ethical questions here are profound: How do we balance public safety against privacy and civil liberties? Already, mass surveillance systems powered by AI are in use in a majority of countries worldwide. Even some democratic societies have rapidly adopted AI surveillance technologies, raising concerns about potential overreach. A particularly sensitive issue is real-time facial recognition in public places – an AI system that can identify individuals in a crowd could help catch criminals or find missing persons, but it could just as easily be misused to track citizens, target minority communities, or stifle dissent. These concerns are not hypothetical; in fact, they have prompted ethical stands from within the tech industry. For instance, the president of one leading technology company publicly called for government regulation of facial recognition to prevent abuse, and another major firm went so far as to stop offering its facial recognition software to law enforcement, citing the risk of facilitating human rights violations. Such actions underscore that even the creators of AI are wary of how their products might be misapplied in surveillance contexts. For managers, the challenge is to navigate these tools responsibly: if deploying AI for security (say, in a corporate campus or retail setting), it's crucial to implement strict usage policies and ensure compliance with privacy laws and norms. At the same time, the opportunity is that AI, when applied with a "privacy-first" design, can enhance safety without infringing on rights. A real-world example comes from a recent public safety project in which police partnered with researchers to manage event crowds using AI analysis without invasive surveillance. Instead of identifying individuals, the system analyzed video feed data in aggregate – representing people as anonymous dots on a map – to detect crowd surges and predict bottlenecks. This privacy-preserving approach allowed authorities to respond to safety hazards in real time while respecting individual anonymity. Such cases illustrate a broader point: AI for social good is most powerful when it thrives on ethical design. Whether it's healthcare AI that is carefully audited for fairness across patient groups, or climate AI that shares data transparently with affected communities, the emerging opportunity is to use AI as a tool to augment human decision-making for positive outcomes. If done right, AI systems can help humans overcome our biases and blind spots – for example, diagnosing diseases more equitably or allocating resources based on data rather than prejudice – thereby improving societal outcomes.

In summary, the road ahead is rife with new AI-driven challenges, from hallucinating chatbots to biased hiring algorithms and watchful sensors, each posing questions about truth, fairness, and privacy. Yet, in confronting these issues head-on, ethical managers can unlock parallel opportunities. AI tools can be harnessed to reduce human error and bias, provided we insist on careful design and oversight. And AI can be steered towards socially beneficial uses – improving health, safety, and environment – if we commit to the ethical principles that ensure technology serves humanity and not the other way around.

The Changing Regulatory Landscape

The ethical environment around AI is not just shaped by corporate values and customer expectations – increasingly, it is also being defined by laws and regulations. Around the world, governments are beginning to grapple with how to rein in the risks of AI while still encouraging innovation. For managers, this means that the coming years will likely bring new rules that impact AI projects, from data handling to algorithmic transparency. Rather than seeing this as a compliance burden alone, business leaders should recognize it as a chance to standardize good practices and build trust with the public.

A leading example is the European Union's AI Act, slated to be one of the first comprehensive legal frameworks for AI. The EU AI Act establishes a risk-based classification for AI systems, imposing different rules depending on an AI application's potential impact. At the highest end, a handful of AI uses are deemed "unacceptable risk" and will be outright banned once the law comes into effect. These include things like AI that engages in manipulative behavior targeting vulnerable groups, government-run social scoring systems (scoring citizens' trustworthiness like some dystopian credit score), or omnipresent real-time facial recognition in public spaces. The message from regulators is clear: certain uses of AI are considered so harmful to fundamental rights and democratic values that they have no place in a principled business strategy. Just below this tier, the law defines "high-risk" AI systems – typically applications that affect people's safety or critical life opportunities. This category covers AI used in areas such as employment and HR (hiring algorithms, worker monitoring systems), education (like scoring student essays), essential public services, law enforcement decisions, and more. Companies deploying AI in these high-impact domains will face strict requirements: before such a system hits the market, it must undergo thorough risk assessments, and throughout its lifecycle it will need to comply with governance practices like logging decisions, ensuring human oversight, and enabling audits. Notably, the EU Act also gives the public a voice – people will have the right to file complaints or seek explanations for decisions made by high-risk AI. What does this mean for a manager? If your company's AI is, say, screening loan applications or tracking productivity, you may soon be legally obliged to provide transparency and accountability measures by design. While that might sound daunting, it can actually professionalize the field – much as financial reporting or data privacy laws forced organizations to adopt uniform best practices.

Even AI applications that are not considered high-risk won't be entirely off the regulatory radar. The EU (and likely others following its lead) is also introducing transparency obligations for general AI systems that interact with consumers. A case in point: generative AI models like chatbots or AI image generators will be required to disclose that their content is AI-generated, to prevent confusion or deception. They'll also need to implement safeguards against illicit content and respect intellectual property rights – for example, developers may have to publish summaries of copyrighted material used in training data. If we imagine a near-future scenario, it's not far-fetched that any AI system affecting customers might come with an "AI ethics label", much like a nutrition label on food. Such a label would inform users about the AI's core ingredients: where the training data came from, how the algorithm was tested for bias, what level of human oversight is present, and so on. This kind of transparency is exactly what many regulators are aiming for. In fact, forward-thinking companies have already begun experimenting with AI transparency labels. One enterprise software firm recently introduced an internal requirement that every new generative AI product must include an "AI Nutrition Facts" style report before launch. Much like a food label lists calories and vitamins, this AI factsheet details which large language model is used, how customer data is handled, what the system's limitations are, and the intended ethical safeguards. By making such a label a standard part of development, the company ensures that key ethical questions (bias, privacy, accountability) are addressed up front rather than as an afterthought. Early reactions from clients and stakeholders have been positive – the transparency not only helps users trust the AI more, but also sparks productive conversations about how it should (and shouldn't) be used. This real-world example provides a glimpse of what broader regulation might bring: an ecosystem where transparency and disclosure are the norm, and where users can easily compare AI systems based on standardized ethical criteria.

It's also worth noting that public expectations are rising alongside formal regulations. Consumers and civil society are increasingly vocal that AI should be explainable, fair, and respectful of privacy. Failing to meet these expectations can result in reputational damage or loss of business, even if laws don't yet mandate certain practices. In one illustrative analogy, ethical AI advocates have suggested an "ethics label" on AI products – akin to organic or fair-trade stickers – to signal to customers that a system has been vetted for responsible use. We may soon see something like this become reality, either through industry self-regulation or as part of compliance regimes. Rather than resisting these changes, businesses can embrace them as an opportunity. Clear rules can actually level the playing field by setting minimum standards that every competitor must follow, preventing the race-to-the-bottom scenario where the least scrupulous players undercut others. If a law requires, for example, algorithmic bias testing and documentation, then investing in those processes no longer puts a company at a disadvantage – instead, it becomes the norm and fosters trust across the board. Progressive managers are already thinking this way: some have even actively supported sensible AI regulations, recognizing that sound rules can enhance innovation by building public confidence. After all, when users have confidence that AI systems are audited and transparent, they are more likely to adopt and benefit from them.

In sum, the regulatory landscape for AI is quickly evolving, with major initiatives like the EU AI Act heralding a new era of "ethical compliance". Managers should stay informed about these developments and see them not just as boxes to tick, but as a roadmap for best practices.

Envision a future where whenever your company rolls out an AI-driven service, you can proudly present its ethics credentials – how it was built responsibly and in line with the latest standards. Preparing for that future now will not only keep you ahead of the law but also strengthen your brand's credibility in the eyes of customers and partners.

Ethical Leadership and Innovation

As we look to the road ahead, one encouraging theme emerges: ethical AI isn't just a moral imperative, it's also good business. Companies that lead with principles and prioritize digital ethics are finding that this approach builds deeper trust with customers, employees, and partners – trust which increasingly translates into a competitive advantage. In an age of data-driven services, trust is currency. A business known for safeguarding user data, avoiding harmful biases, and being transparent about its AI will attract loyal customers and face fewer PR crises. Ethical leadership in AI thus becomes a strategic asset, not a hindrance.

Real-world examples are already bearing this out. One global consumer goods corporation found success by positioning itself as a model of transparency in data and AI use. This company made its privacy and AI data policies extremely clear and accessible to the public, ensuring customers understand exactly how their information is collected and used. By proactively communicating its ethical guidelines, it earned consumers' trust and was able to roll out highly personalized AI-driven marketing campaigns that were well-received, knowing customers were comfortable with how their data was handled. Another example comes from a major retailer in the beauty industry that deployed an AI-driven virtual makeup advisor. From the start, the company focused on inclusivity – they trained the AI on diverse facial data so that the tool would work equally well for all skin tones and ethnic features, and they were upfront about what data was being collected and why. The result was a popular app that not only delivered useful recommendations but also enhanced the brand's reputation for diversity and respect. Users who might have been skeptical of an algorithm advising them on personal style felt reassured by the brand's openness and the evident care put into making the AI fair for everyone. These cases illustrate how ethical AI practices can enhance customer trust and business effectiveness at the same time. Customers are more likely to engage with and remain loyal to services when they feel their values are being respected.

Ethical leadership in AI also resonates strongly with business partners and regulators, which can open doors for collaboration and market access. For instance, enterprise clients (especially in sectors like finance or healthcare) often conduct due diligence on vendors' AI ethics. If your company can demonstrate that your algorithms are audited for bias, your data is secured, and your outcomes are explainable, that credibility can win you contracts over a competitor with a spottier record. In this way, being principled in AI use becomes part of your value proposition. One might even market it: we've seen firms publicly advertise their adoption of "AI ethics charters" or certifications, signaling to the world that they uphold certain standards. Far from being marketing fluff, these claims, when backed by real action, make a substantive difference. They reduce the risk for clients and consumers in using AI-driven products and thus become a selling point.

Crucially, committing to ethics does not mean stifling innovation – in fact, it can spur innovation. When teams must solve for ethical constraints, they often come up with novel solutions that push the technology forward in a positive direction. Take the challenge of explainability. Complex AI models (like deep neural networks) are often "black boxes" that even their creators struggle to interpret. But demand for responsible AI has driven a wave of research into explainable AI (XAI) techniques – from visualization tools to simplified surrogate models – that can shed light on how AI makes decisions. This push has yielded practical tools such as model cards (documents that accompany an AI model detailing its intended use, performance, and limitations) and open-source libraries for interpretability. A notable innovation is the development of AI factsheets by one tech company – essentially a plain-language report for each AI system, ensuring that developers document how the system works and what data it uses. What began as an effort to increase transparency has, in turn, improved the quality of the AI models; developers report that by having to fill out a factsheet, they catch potential issues early and think more deeply about their design choices. Another domain is privacy. The ethical mandate to protect user data has inspired techniques like differential privacy and federated learning, which were cutting-edge academic concepts only a few years ago and are now becoming industry standards. *Differential privacy*, for example, adds mathematical noise to data analyses so that no individual's information can be pinpointed – this allows organizations to glean insights from large datasets while rigorously safeguarding personal privacy. *Federated learning,* likewise, enables training machine learning models across multiple data sources (like hospitals or smartphones) without ever aggregating the raw data in one place. These innovations mean that companies can collaborate on AI development (say, building a more accurate health diagnostic model across hospitals globally) without exposing sensitive data, thus achieving a leap in capability that would be impossible if privacy concerns hadn't forced a new approach. In short, solving ethical challenges often drives technical creativity. The need for fairness has prompted new algorithms for bias detection and synthetic data generation to balance datasets. The need for accountability has led to ideas like algorithmic audit trails and monitoring systems that log AI decisions for later review. Each of these not only addresses an ethical requirement but also adds to the robustness and reliability of AI systems.

From a leadership perspective, reframing ethics as a fuel for innovation rather than a brake on it is powerful. It sets a tone where teams see constraints as a puzzle to spark creativity. Managers can encourage this by celebrating ethical "wins" – for example, highlighting how an AI product became more inclusive after incorporating user feedback, or how building with privacy in mind won over a key client segment. Over time, such an environment attracts talent too. Many AI professionals, from data scientists to engineers, want to work at companies that align with their values and use technology for good. A reputation for principled decision-making in AI can thus help a business recruit and retain top-tier employees who are motivated to innovate responsibly.

To encapsulate, ethical leadership in AI is a competitive differentiator. Companies that nurture an ethical culture and invest in responsible AI are effectively future-proofing their business – they minimize the risk of scandals, fines, and customer backlash, while maximizing trust and long-term sustainability. And as a pleasant surprise, they may find that the very act of wrestling with ethical questions leads them to better AI solutions. When ethics is baked into the design process, the end product tends to be more thoughtful, user-aligned, and innovative. In the data-driven world ahead, the winners will likely be those who prove that you can do well by doing good – leveraging principled decisions as the foundation for technological and business success.

Commitment to Ongoing Learning

Perhaps the most important realization for any manager navigating AI is that the journey of ethical AI is never "finished." Technology, business contexts, and societal expectations are all evolving so rapidly that staying ethical is a continuous process of learning, adjusting, and improving. A policy or understanding that was sufficient last year might become outdated next year with the advent of a new AI capability or a new regulation. Therefore, a key principle for the road ahead is a commitment to ongoing learning – both at the individual level and the organizational level.

No one – not even AI experts – has all the answers in this fast-changing field. Staying curious and engaged is critical. Managers and professionals can foster this by actively seeking out resources and forums that discuss AI ethics. For instance, consider attending AI ethics workshops or training programs that are now increasingly offered by universities, industry groups, and professional associations. These can range from short courses on topics like "ethical machine learning" to certification programs in responsible AI governance. Some forward-looking companies have begun to require such training internally; one North American bank, for example, established a dedicated data ethics team and made it mandatory for all employees in data analytics roles to complete annual ethics training as part of the company's code of conduct. This kind of initiative ensures that knowledge and awareness of issues (like bias, privacy, and compliance requirements) remain fresh and top-of-mind for those working with AI day-to-day.

Managers should also look beyond their own organization's walls for learning opportunities. Participating in industry-wide consortia and networks focused on AI ethics can be incredibly valuable. Groups such as multi-company partnerships, think tanks, or standards bodies allow professionals to share best practices and even develop common frameworks. By joining these conversations, a manager can learn from peers – for example, how another firm conducted an algorithmic bias audit or implemented an AI transparency report – and bring those insights back home. Such collaboration can prevent each company from having to reinvent the wheel on ethical guidelines. It also helps harmonize approaches, which is useful when regulators or global partners are looking for consistency.

Another powerful idea is to nurture an internal culture of ethical dialogue. One way to do this is by setting up an internal "AI ethics forum" or working group. This might involve a periodic meeting (say monthly or quarterly) where people from diverse departments – IT, legal, HR, product development, etc. – come together to discuss current events or dilemmas in AI. They could review new guidelines, debate a recent AI controversy in the news, or assess an ongoing project through an ethical lens. By making this a regular practice, ethical reflection becomes "baked in" to the organization's operations. It encourages employees to speak up if they foresee a concern and creates a space to resolve ambiguities. In practice, companies have taken various approaches: some have appointed ethics champions or councils at the executive level, while others empower grassroots committees. The common thread is to keep the conversation alive. As one expert noted, organizations need to ensure teams and individuals are engaged with AI ethics as part of their everyday work, not as an abstract annual concern. When ethical considerations become part of daily decision-making – from design meetings to marketing strategy – the company is far less likely to be blindsided by an AI mishap.

In embracing continuous learning, it's helpful to remember that ethical AI is a journey, not a destination. The technology will keep improving, and new situations will arise that have no clear precedent. This means adaptability is key. Managers should remain open to updating policies and practices as new knowledge comes in. For example, if new research reveals a previously unknown bias in a popular algorithm, a responsive organization would revisit its models and retrain or adjust them accordingly. If a new law is passed, an agile team will quickly educate itself on the requirements and integrate them into the project workflow. Flexibility and willingness to learn are what separate companies that merely comply with ethics from those that truly lead with ethics.

Here are a few concrete steps and habits managers can cultivate to stay on the cutting edge of ethical AI:

- **Engage with the AI ethics community:** Follow relevant journals, blogs, or conferences. Joining forums or attending conferences (even virtually) such as those by the IEEE or the Partnership on AI can keep you informed about the latest ethical challenges and solutions being discussed globally.

- **Encourage team education:** Sponsor your employees to attend ethics workshops or bring in experts for seminars. Encourage key staff to acquire certifications (for instance, in AI governance or data privacy) and share their learnings with the team.

- **Set up internal review processes:** Establish a practice where new AI initiatives go through an ethics review. This could be a simple checklist or a formal committee, depending on the scale of the project. The idea is to consciously pause and evaluate potential impacts – a habit that reinforces learning by doing.

- **Learn from incidents (yours and others'):** If something goes wrong – say an AI system produces a biased outcome or a customer complains about an AI-driven service – treat it as a learning opportunity. Do a post-mortem analysis, identify what could prevent that issue, and update your guidelines. Likewise, keep an eye on public AI incidents and discuss them internally: "Could that happen to us? How would we respond?" These scenario exercises can be invaluable.

Finally, remember that you are not alone on this road. The ethical AI community is growing, and it thrives on collaboration and shared progress. Governments, academia, and industry are all investing in resources to help navigate these waters – from open-source toolkits to ethical frameworks. Tapping into those resources will make your journey easier. And importantly, lead by example: when your organization demonstrates a commitment to doing the right thing with AI, it adds to the collective momentum. Your leadership might inspire another, creating a ripple effect that improves practices across your sector.

To conclude this chapter – and this book's exploration of human-centered AI – keep in mind that making principled decisions is an ongoing voyage. There won't be a point where one can sit back and say, "We've nailed ethics in AI, nothing more to do." Instead, successful, human-centered organizations will be those that continue asking questions, continue learning, and continue adapting as the data-driven world unfolds. *No one has all the answers in this evolving field, but by staying proactive and curious, you can ensure your organization navigates the future of AI with integrity and purpose.* In doing so, you will uphold your values while harnessing the best of AI innovation – truly thriving in the age of AI, not in spite of ethical constraints, but because of your principled approach.

Epilogue

Our journey through the terrain of ethical artificial intelligence has revealed both the complexity and the promise of managing technology with human values at its core. Managers today stand at a decisive crossroads: the choices made in how algorithms are designed, deployed, and governed will not only shape business outcomes but also leave lasting imprints on society.

The central message of this book has been consistent—ethics is not an optional layer added once systems are already in motion. It is a foundation, a guiding compass that aligns innovation with fairness, accountability, and trust. Leaders who commit to principled decision-making gain more than compliance or reputation; they gain resilience, agility, and enduring relevance in an era when transparency and responsibility are watched closely by stakeholders and customers alike.

AI has already demonstrated the power to accelerate decisions, scale insights, and open new opportunities. Yet its greatest potential lies in enabling a future where technology does not eclipse humanity, but elevates it. From bias audits and governance frameworks to inclusive design and global standards, the tools and principles outlined in these pages provide managers with a practical roadmap. The next step requires courage—the courage to prioritize integrity even when efficiency tempts, to question systems that appear neutral but carry unseen bias, and to design with the conviction that dignity must never be traded for speed.

Looking forward, the possibilities are immense. As organizations embrace human-centered AI, they can pioneer a business culture where ethics and profitability reinforce each other. The data-driven age does not have to diminish our humanity; with intention and leadership, it can expand it. The opportunity now is to build systems that reflect not only intelligence but also wisdom—technology guided by the best of human values, creating progress that is as principled as it is powerful.